Hurry Up and Fail

How Success Rises from the Ashes of Failure

By Dave Mason

Copyright © 2023 by Dave Mason

All Rights Reserved

All the people and stories depicted in this book are true and accurate to the best of my knowledge, with the exception of Elon Musk, who I believe is actually building Space X to send himself home. Thank you for all the gifts you bestowed upon humanity during your brief stay on Earth, Elon. Safe travels back to wherever you came from.

I wrote this book to be used, so feel free to cite it, quote from it, and teach from small excerpts. Just do not claim it as your own, sell it, or make a pirated audiobook (as someone did with my book The Size of Your Dreams).

Cover design by the amazing Juan Hernaz.
Check out his other amazing works at JuanHernaz.com.

Interior layout by Zoran Maksimović, macsimovic@gmail.com

Cartoons by Eduardo Comoglio

In memory of my maternal grandparents,
Lee and Evelyn Diamond,
whose story is touched upon within these pages.

*Thank you for always believing in me
and teaching me the value of work and play.*

Contents

Introduction — 9

Part 1: Why Failure? — 13
Chapter 1: Embrace Failure — 15

Part 2: Hurry up and Fail — 25
Chapter 2: Lower the Stakes — 27
Chapter 3: Start Before You're Ready — 31
Chapter 4: Fail Fast, Fail Cheap — 39
Chapter 5: Learn to Love Rejection — 51
Chapter 6: Fail Small, Fail Often — 61

Part 3: Learning from Failure — 71
Chapter 7: Seek Feedback — 73
Chapter 8: Investigate Failure — 83
Chapter 9: Forsee Failure — 93

Part 4: Mitigating Failure — 107

Chapter 10: Protect Your Downside — 109
Chapter 11: Build Early Warning Systems — 117
Chapter 12: Heed the Signs — 121
Chapter 13: Quit like a Champion — 129

Part 5: Don't Fail on Others — 137

Chapter 14: Own Your Failures — 139
Chapter 15: Exceed Expectations — 145
Chapter 16: Nurture Belonging — 151

Epilogue — 157

Acknowledgments — 160
Notes — 161
About the Author — 167
Other books by Dave Mason — 168
The Size of Your Dreams sample — 171

Two Quick Notes Before You Begin

1. Part of the *Hurry Up and Fail* philosophy is to gather feedback and continually make improvements. If there's an idea you find confusing, or a concept you'd like more elaboration on, or (Heaven forbid) a typo, let me know at DaveMasonAuthor.com/fail.

2. Want to assess your own ability to *Hurry Up and Fail*? Identify your own failure blindspots by taking our Failure Scorecard at DaveMasonAuthor.com/failure-scorecard. It's totally free and should take you no more than ten minutes to complete.

You can also access the feedback form and
the Failure Scorecard by scanning the QR code below:

DaveMasonAuthor.com/fail

Introduction

In January 2019, my wife Chana and I traveled to the edge of the Ecuadorian rainforest, where we filmed a course based on our book *The Size of Your Dreams*. But the video clips from Ecuador never saw the light of day, and all our careful preparations were wasted. Why? Because we feared the finished product wouldn't meet our meticulous standards.

Fast forward a year and a half to May 2020. After repeatedly failing to film the ideal course, we stopped aiming for perfection. Rather than continuing to hone our script, we threw the script out the window. Instead of filming in a studio or another remote destination, we used our webcam. Most importantly, we didn't launch a completed course; we taught our materials live.

On the first night of *Dream, Design, Manifest*, I stood in front of over fifty participants and, with trepidation, informed them we had no idea what we were doing. I told them about our disastrous attempt to film in Ecuador and our inability to move forward since. "We're going to *Hurry Up and Fail*," I said, and offer whatever we have.

I braced myself. Our students had good reason to be upset. After all, they'd paid a significant amount to join this course, and now their teachers were admitting to *winging it*. But I wasn't prepared for their reaction. Rather than booing or asking for their money back, the group cheered. Indeed, *Hurry Up and Fail*, a phrase I'd created on the spot, became a rallying cry during the six-week course. Participants made bold moves and bragged on group boards about their failures with the hashtag #Hurryupandfail.

Much has been written about the Science of Success. It sounds strange to discuss the Science of Failure, but that's exactly what this book is about. We all know the road to success is paved with failures, but not all failures are created equal. While some serve as springboards to achieve greater heights, other leave us broken and unwilling to continue.

In this book, we'll examine the key elements of successful failures. We'll delve into famous fiascos by the likes of Elon Musk and Sir Richard Branson, as well as some not-so-famous failures, each time unearthing the teachings buried within. In Part 1, we'll delve into our understanding of what constitutes success and failure. We'll address our mental blocks around failure so that, in Part 2, we can examine ways to fail faster and more effectively. Failing fast can accelerate our learning process, but only if we know how to learn from our blunders, so in Part 3 we'll unpack ways to most effectively learn from failure.

Of course, learning from defeats is fine when they don't cause significant harm. In Parts 4 and 5, we'll explore how to mitigate the negative effects of our failures, with Part 4 focused on reducing the impact on ourselves and our businesses and Part 5 highlighting how to protect our customers or innocent bystanders from the consequences of our failures. By the time we're through, I hope to empower you with enough distinctions to help you turn losses into gains so you can rapidly move from failure to success.

Without further ado, let us Hurry Up and Fail!

PART 1

Why Failure?

CHAPTER 1

Embrace Failure

"I have not failed. I've just found ten thousand ways that do not work."

- THOMAS EDISON

Sara Blakely sat across from Diane, a Neiman Marcus hosiery buyer, watching the opportunity of a lifetime slip away. The year was 2000, and the buyer only grudgingly gave Sara ten minutes of her time because Sara had flown in for the meeting. But Diane was unimpressed by the 29-year-old, self-proclaimed inventor who'd shown up to Neiman Marcus headquarters with her battered, lucky red backpack, a color photocopy of her packaging, and her only prototype in a ziplock bag. After selling fax machines for the last seven years, Sara had enough experience with prospects shredding her business card to recognize disinterest when she saw it. She tried one last, desperate attempt to win over the buyer before her ten-minute opportunity lapsed. "Diane," Sara said, "will you come with me to the bathroom?"

"Excuse me?" Despite sitting through thousands of such meetings, Diane had never met such a request.

"I know, I know. It's a little weird," Sara said. "Will you just please come with me to the bathroom?"

Diane ignored her misgivings and agreed.

Sara wore the same extravagant, $98 cream-colored pants she'd worn the night she had her inspiration two years earlier. These pants had caused her fits because they were thin, unlined, and showed far too much of her underwear for comfort. So despite costing a considerable amount of money, they'd hung in her closet unworn. Then one night, she had an idea. She took a pair of control-top pantyhose, cut off the feet, and viola. The ugly panty lines disappeared.

Sara showed Diane how horrible her butt looked with a pair of ordinary panties beneath her cream pants. Then she went into a stall, took her prototype out of its ziplock bag, put it on, and came out to demonstrate her new, improved look.

Diane looked at Sara as if seeing her for the first time. "Wow. I get it. It's brilliant. I'm going to place an order, and I'm going to put it in seven stores and see how it goes."

These days, a purchase needs to cost significantly more than $98 to be extravagant in Sara's eyes, such as her purchasing a stake in the NBA's Atlanta Hawks in 2015. Only three years earlier, Forbes had declared her the world's youngest self-made female billionaire. Spanx, the company she built out of those cutoff pantyhose, became a gigantic success.

"Build a better mousetrap, and the world will beat a path to your door," is a famous business quotation attributed to Ralph Waldo Emerson (though it's not precisely what he said). The Spanx story is a great example of the "better mousetrap" principle. Sara Blakely redesigned ladies' undergarments in a way that made her clients' clothing look better. She produced a better product, and the world beat a path to her door, just as the adage promised.

Except the deeper you dig into Sara's story, the more the mousetrap theory falls apart.

Innovative as Sara's solution was, it was hardly original. Countless women later told Sara they'd been cutting off the feet of their own pantyhose years before Spanx came along. So how come Sara became a billionaire and the rest of the women just wound up with frayed, footless pantyhose?

When learning Sara's story, my mind kept traveling back to my maternal grandparents, who lived in an age where gender roles were practically set in stone. My grandfather, however, was a nurturer at heart, and my grandmother a businesswoman. They started to thrive financially when Grandmom left homemaking to open a series of women's clothing stores, ultimately pulling in Grandpop in a supporting role.

On visits to Philadelphia as a kid, I'd hurry through the sales floor of *Suzanne's*, passing hundreds of dresses, blouses, and undergarments, to run to Grandpop's desk. Looking back, I'm not exactly sure what my grandfather did; I mostly remember him taking me out to lunch. Likely, he helped with business operations and ran the back office. But the unquestionable powerhouse at *Suzanne's* was Grandmom, who bought the inventory, ran the showroom, and outfitted customers.

Embrace Failure

My experience with my grandparents probably skewed my perceptions of women's apparel. While I knew the business world is male dominated, I thought surely if there were any industry where enterprising women like my grandmother had made serious inroads, it would be in women's attire. And if there were any subcategory within that market where women must dominate, it *had* to be undergarments, that most intimate category, where only those who wore them could possibly know how they felt.

But, as you've probably guessed, that's not what Sara discovered. She found an industry run entirely by men, all stuck in their ways, unwilling to hear a woman's opinion about how to move forward. It's not like Sara was begging. She had money. Not a ton, but enough to fund the production of her new product. But even with cash in hand, all the manufacturers she approached turned her down.

Sara was nothing if not persistent. She kept knocking on doors until she found one manufacturer willing to reconsider. What made him different? It wasn't that he thought Sara had a good idea. He thought she was crazy. But he ran the concept past his daughters, who pushed him to move forward. He gave Sara a shot, more out of kindness than business interest, as evidenced by his stunned silence when Neiman Marcus placed their first order. He later confided to Sara he thought she'd be stuck giving away her remaining inventory as Christmas gifts for years to come.

But finding a willing manufacturer wasn't the end of the story, not by a long shot. Before the cut-off hose could be made, she had battles to fight over product design and materials. After all that, she had thousands of dollars in inventory of a product no one had ever heard about, and according to most market experts, no one even wanted.

Sara says one of the biggest mistakes entrepreneurs make is declaring victory once they receive their first big purchase order. To her, getting Neiman Marcus to put her product on their shelves was only a partial victory; and one that masked a potentially disastrous pitfall.

What was the pitfall? Imagine for a moment that Sara filled the Neiman purchase order, sent off the product, then turned her attention to securing her next contract. The sales reps in the hosiery department would have received a product they'd never heard of and didn't know how to sell. Customers wouldn't request the product because they didn't know it existed. Most likely, Spanx would have languished on the shelves for a few months before Neiman wrote the experiment off as a dud and returned the unsold inventory. Sara's big break could have been the end of her company.

But this brazen inventor realized it was up to her to ensure her product's success. She called everyone she knew who lived in a city where Spanx was now sold. She recounts these phone calls as going something like, "Hi, it's Sara. Remember me from fourth grade? Do you mind going to the store and buying Spanx, and I'll send you a check?"

Send them a check? Wasn't the entire point of selling Spanx to be making money? Eventually, yes. But first she had to prove there was a market. And since there wasn't one, she had to create it.

Sara hit the road for an education campaign. She went to each Neiman Marcus store and showcased it to sales reps. But not just to those in the hosiery department. She also hit the shoe department. Why shoes? Because no one wants to wear open-toed shoes with panty hose, and if the shoe staff understood the advantages of Spanx, it could help them increase their sales and commissions.

But Sara didn't stop there. She bought cheap plastic display racks, loaded them with Spanx, and placed them by checkout registers. It was such a bold, unprecedented move that she initially received little pushback. Why? Because everyone just assumed she had the authority to do it.

Ultimately, complaints reached the Neiman Marcus CEO about this woman who kept entering stores and engaging in unauthorized activities. To his credit, before acting on the complaints, he looked up her products. By this time, she'd reached a million dollars in sales, and the CEO responded, "Whatever this woman is doing seems to be working, so let her keep doing it."

We've just scratched the surface of Sara's legendary exploits on her road to success. While still handling all inventory and shipping out of her apartment, before she'd even built a website, she got Spanx in Oprah's hands, who named it one of her favorite products of the year. Sara got Spanx on QVC, a shopping channel famous for its discounted goods, yet she refused to offer their customers even a single penny off the retail price and still sold out all 8000 units in six minutes. Her willingness to take chances didn't stop with Spanx, as evidenced by her climb up the side of a hot air balloon, while it flew 10,000 feet in the air, to meet eccentric billionaire Richard Branson for tea.

While taking an entrepreneurship class Sara teaches on Masterclass.com, I reflected on my career as an author. Like Sara, I've always wanted complete ownership of my products and ideas. I've received multiple offers from publishers for my books, but I've always self-published to maintain full control. Unlike Sara, though, I've taken a half-assed approach to marketing my books. Watching her Masterclass, I told my wife, "If Sara had written our books, she would have found a way to make them runaway bestsellers."

So how did she do it? How did she become a billionaire with a product modification that wasn't even an original idea? In her own words, "I've never taken a business class in my life, I had no contacts in the industry, and I took on billion dollar companies with $5000. So I would say mindset is pretty much it."

It's no surprise to hear an indomitable mindset is key to success. The real question is how can we mere mortals cultivate such a powerful mindset?

James emerged from the hospital unable to stand, much less walk. He struggled to coordinate the movements of the left side of his body with his right. His family knew it would be many years until he could hope to live independently, and they'd have to attend to his most basic needs day and night.

But James was determined. A year out of the hospital, he could finally stand on his own, though he often had to hold on to tables or chairs for support. Walking was a different story. In one short hour, he fell 71 times. But each time, he picked himself up and tried again.

Before long, James could walk as well as any of us. Because, ultimately, James is one of us. James wasn't hospitalized for a car accident or a stroke. He'd emerged from the hospital at the tender age of two days old.

You too started life incapable of doing pretty much anything. You couldn't walk or talk or sleep through the night. You made a mess when you ate and pooped your pants.

Were you mocked for your repeated failures? Were you told you were a loser who'd never amount to anything? Not likely. You were cheered on, encouraged. And if you can walk today, it's only because you tried and tried and tried again until you mastered the skill, undaunted by your blunders.

Everything you now do well, you once did poorly.

Human beings are learning machines. Every child has an insatiable desire to learn, grow, and master new skills. We fail millions of times along the way, and we just don't care. When we're little, we embrace it.

But somewhere along the line, all that changes.

I remember a conversation from a carpool just before 9th grade. My friend's mother asked what classes I was planning on taking. When she heard the list of honors classes I'd signed up for, she shook her head. "To get into a good college, you want to have as strong a GPA (Grade Point Average) as possible, so you're better off taking the easiest classes you can."

My friend, sitting shotgun, nodded along to his mother's words, then told me his own class choices. Sure enough, at the end of the semester when our grades came back, his GPA trounced my own, and this strategy gave him a significant leg up when it came time to apply to college. But did it make him a better student?

Hurry Up and Fail

Let's take a more extreme example. Max and Tina enter high school at polar opposite ends of the spectrum. Max gets straight A's from day one. He barely exerts himself in school, putting in minimal effort to get 90% or above on his exams.

Tina starts 9th grade barely able to read and squeaks by with a D average. But Tina is sick of feeling like the dumb kid. She stays late after school for extra tutoring. Her friends help her with reading on the weekends. The following year, she manages a C average, in 11th grade a B, and by 12th grade she's right alongside Max scoring A's in every class.

Between Max and Tina, who's likely to get into the better college? It's not even close. Max can apply to Ivy League schools with his 4.0 GPA. Tina's GPA would only average a 2.5 across her four years of school, not high enough for top universities to even consider her.

But if I were to bet on one of their futures, I'd take Tina hands down. Not only is her performance at the end of high school on par with Max's, she also showed grit, determination, and a willingness to learn and grow that Max lacked. But the grading and ranking systems we employ don't encourage growth; they penalize it.

What a crazy system. Most of us understand at a deep level that failure is part of the learning process. If the goal of school is to learn, then we should be rewarded for pushing ourselves to the edge of our comfort level. But our education system ingrains the opposite message, that every time we step outside our comfort zone, we risk getting a poor grade, which can lower our GPA, and hurt our chances of advancing. Is it any wonder most of us leave school terrified of failing?

Let's return to Sara Blakely. How could she take so many steps that would intimidate most anyone else? She traces the roots of her resilience back to her father.

When sitting around the dinner table, Sara's father would regularly ask his children, "How did you fail this week?" He wasn't giving his kids a hard time about their mishaps. Just the opposite. He encouraged them to feel proud for trying something difficult and failing in the attempt.

"I didn't realize it at the time," Sara says, "but he was changing my definition of failure. My definition of failure became not about the outcome, but about not trying. So for me, going through life, my only failures are when I didn't try because I was scared."

Embrace Failure

But Sara's father didn't stop there. "My Dad even took it a step further. He would ask us what benefit we got or what positive came from it."

In Sara's house, failure was interwoven with adventure and learning. Some of you may consider this a given. If so, you're ahead of the game. As Sara explains, "Why is our biggest fear as human beings the fear of failure? It's because we don't want to be embarrassed...Fear of what other people think of me is the real root of the issue."

When I told people I was writing a book called *Hurry up and Fail*, some asked, "Why failure? Why not hurry up and succeed? Why not hurry up and take action? Why harp on *failure* of all things?"

At the heart of the *Hurry up and Fail* ethos is this same understanding of the power of language and our personal narratives that Sara Blakely's father used to help his daughter become a billionaire. If we reframe our definition of the word failure and the stories we tell about our gaffes, the fear of failure will no longer rule over us.

To achieve that reframing, we need to shift our perception of failure from something we run away from to something we want to run *towards*. So how do we do this if we didn't grow up with a father like Sara's?

Recently, I wanted to get back into the stock market. Even though I'd had some success at picking stocks earlier in my life, I had one tragic flaw that ruined it. Whenever I'd buy a stock that dropped, I'd freeze. I couldn't handle the shame of making a bad pick. Rather than selling it, taking my losses, and moving on, I'd hang onto it, hoping it would miraculously turn around. The further it crashed, the less I'd check my portfolio, not wanting to face my one awful decision. Eventually, my portfolio was bleeding money across the board.

Needless to say, this pattern of ignoring bad decisions is disastrous for stock trading. How could I embrace periodic losses as a cost of doing business and quickly get back in the game? I told my wife I needed a tool to help me make that emotional shift whenever I picked a dud.

We put our heads together and created a Failure playlist on Spotify, including Queen's *Another One Bites the Dust* and *It's the End of the World as We Know It (and I Feel Fine)* by R.E.M. Now, every time I make a bad pick and sell it at a loss, we crank up the Failure playlist and have ourselves a dance party.

To be clear, we're not celebrating our losses. We're celebrating that I showed up and tried my best, that I didn't ignore the botched purchase, but learned from it, and acted fast.

A few short weeks of dance parties helped me drop my negative emotions around these losses by 80% or more. That's enough for me to get back in the game, to no longer fear that I'm going to freeze up when I make a bad investment.

While failure playlists and dance parties are our favorite way of shifting our meaning of failure, there are hundreds of other ways to help yourself make this shift. Before we move on, let's look at a few more:

1. **Bake a failure cake or favorite dessert.** Extra points if you allow yourself to enjoy your favorite dessert only when you fail. If you have a sweet tooth like mine, you'll actually start looking forward to your failings.

2. **Journal about each failure.** For each one, examine what you learned from the experience and what you can improve next time.

3. **Read biographies of successful people.** Once you look beneath the surface, you'll see that everyone who achieved anything great failed over and over again along the way.

4. **Create a failure group.** Form a group which celebrates each member's failures. This can be as simple as an online group where each person shares when they fail and everyone else cheers on their efforts.

5. **Create a failure story slam.** Gather friends and have each tell a funny story about a personal failure. Vote on the best failure story and present a prize to the winner.

6. **Do a physical activity.** Whether you bang out 50 jumping jacks, 20 push ups, or go on a 5 mile run, tying a physical activity to your failures can help you get out of your head and release tension and frustration.

7. **Charitable donations.** Do a kind act each time you fail. Online contributions are fine, but I've found this even more impactful when giving face to face.

In the next section, we'll look at ways to increase, rather than decrease, our failure rate in a way that can accelerate our pace of learning and growth. But first, let's delve further into our understanding of failure, because sometimes a healthy fear of failure can save our lives.

Face your own beliefs around failure
by taking our Failure Scorecard at
DaveMasonAuthor.com/failure-scorecard

PART 2

Hurry up and Fail

CHAPTER 2

Lower the Stakes

"Make failure your teacher, not your undertaker."

—Zig Ziglar

No one claims Everest to be the most beautiful mountain in the world. Nor is it among the more satisfying or difficult technical climbs. Climbers attempt Everest for one reason: it's the highest mountain on Earth.

Everest's peak stands at 29,029 feet above sea level, the cruising altitude of a commercial jet. Helicopters, by comparison, can only reach 25,000 feet before air becomes too thin to keep them airborne. At 26,000 feet, you only get one third of the oxygen as at sea level, making human life unsustainable for any significant period. At this altitude, the cells in our bodies literally start to die, which is why climbers refer to the top 3000 feet of Everest as the Death Zone.

On May 29, 1953, Sir Edmund Hillary and Sherpa Tenzing Norgay became the first two men to reach the peak of Mount Everest (both men refused to reveal who reached the summit first). By this point, more than a dozen men had already died attempting to summit Everest, including George Mallory, the British climber who, when asked why he wanted to reach the world's highest peak, famously quipped, "Because it is there."

The early mountaineers who tried Everest were among the best climbers in the world. But over time, the average skill level of those attempting the climb has gone down. Among the over 300 people who've now died on the face of Everest are quite a few hobbyists, climbers with minimal skills hoping to add their names to the list of those who stood, just for a moment, at the highest point on Earth.

Of course, no hobbyist climber could hope to summit Everest alone. To fill this demand, professional mountaineers have set up companies to guide hobbyists up the mountain. For years, people claimed these guides were tempting fate by bringing up unseasoned climbers. In 1996, fate caught up to them.

Jon Krakauer was covering the climb for *Outsider* magazine and recounts how some members of the expedition had only trained on *StairMasters* rather than on actual mountains and had arrived with brand new hiking boots they'd yet to break in. I won't go into all the horrific details of the climb, but what kept hitting me as I read about the disaster was the long string of bad decisions that contributed to eight climbers failing to make it off the mountain alive, including three trip leaders who were all highly experienced.

Several of their mistakes were simply errors of timing. For instance, they neglected to send off the advance team at the predetermined time to set up the climbing ropes, causing delays during the ascent. When they reached the pre-determined cutoff time, when climbers were supposed to descend whether they'd summited or not, they kept climbing as leaders wanted to give all who paid a chance to reach the top.

The weather brought its own complications. The final ascent to the summit began at midnight on a clear evening with little wind. Dawn broke bright and clear, but by early afternoon, wispy clouds covered the peaks to the south. The clouds looked innocuous enough to the inexperienced eye, especially those unaccustomed to looking at storms from above. But one of the surviving climbers, a pugnacious Texan and long-time pilot named Martin Adams, later recounted to John Krakauer that "he recognized these innocent-looking puffs of water vapor to be the crowns of robust thunderheads immediately after reaching the top. 'When you see a thunderhead in an airplane,' he explained, 'your first reaction is to get the f*ck out of there. So that's what I did.'"

By mid-afternoon, the climbers found themselves in a full-blown storm. Besides bringing high winds and bitter cold, the storm also brought visibility down to nearly zero and erased the tracks the climbers had made on the way up. Indeed, one group simply got lost and failed to find the tents despite successfully navigating their way down to camp elevation.

Then there were physical ailments caused by the altitude. Another Texan, doctor Beck Weathers, suffered so much vision impairment the day before the summit ascent that he could only see a few feet and kept up with the group by stepping in the footprints of the climber ahead of him. Yet, unwilling to give up on his chance for a summit ascent, he kept the severity of his vision impairment to himself and attempted the final climb anyway. As the elevation increased, he found himself blind on the mountainside. His last day of climbing didn't last long, but with no one available to escort him down, he waited on his own most of the day. Later, he descended with the group that couldn't find the tents. While the others died of exposure during the night, Beck somehow survived, though his right hand, all the fingers on his left, and even his nose had to be amputated because of extreme frostbite. He recounts his ordeal in an autobiography entitled *Left for Dead: My Journey Home from Everest*.

Above and beyond the physical challenges of the mountain are the mental ones. In the Death Zone above 26,000 feet, mental processing is notoriously difficult. No doubt mental impairment contributed to several poor decisions made that day, but Jon Krakauer recounts one instance in particular for which he struggles to forgive himself. The first of the team to summit, Jon was already on his way down when he stopped to get himself another oxygen tank from a cache they'd set up in advance. Guide Andy Harris told him all the tanks were empty. Jon tried a tank, found it full, and headed down the mountain. Jon realized Andy's regulator must have frozen, which made him think full tanks were empty. But between Jon's poor processing at that altitude and his natural deference to the guide's authority, he failed to point this out. Andy never worked it out on his own. He not only failed to get extra oxygen for himself, he convinced trip leader Rob Hall and others there was no oxygen available. And neither Andy nor Rob made it down alive.

The Everest disaster of May 11, 1996 is a perfect example of what we are *not* talking about in this book. To summit Everest and make it home alive, many, many things have to go right. One simple mistake, like failing to recognize a frozen regulator is giving inaccurate readings, can lead to multiple deaths.

In a case like climbing Everest, fear of failure can be an extremely healthy thing. Core to the *Hurry Up and Fail* philosophy is that failures are most effective as a tool when they occur quickly and when we take steps to minimize their negative consequences. In the following chapters, we'll dig further into how to engineer our failures so they become low-risk, high-reward learning experiences.

Until then, stay off Everest.

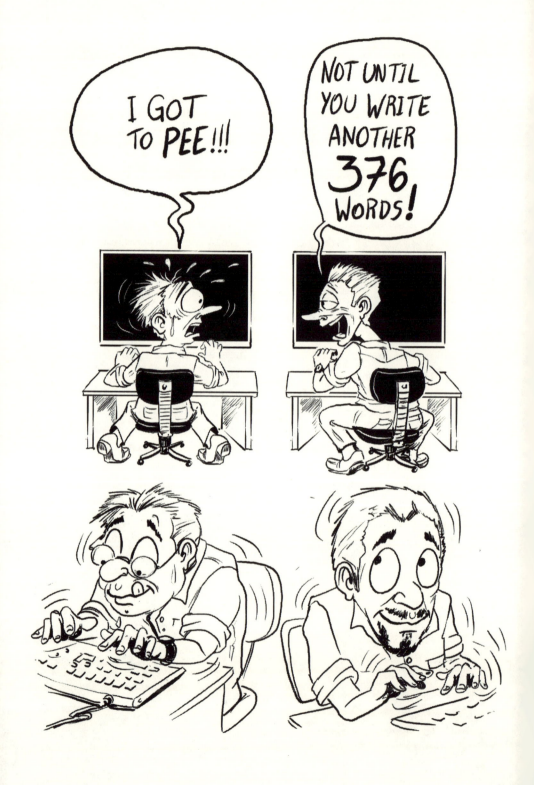

CHAPTER 3

Start Before You're Ready

"If you don't try at anything, you can't fail... it takes back bone to lead the life you want."

—RICHARD YATES

The Sociology Department at Brigham Young University had a shortage of professors during their summer term. This was in the late 1960s, long before the US had a glut of academics with PhDs scrambling to fill a handful of college teaching positions, and BYU struggled to find qualified candidates to cover for two of its professors on summer break.

Help came from an unlikely source; a downed airline pilot. Dr. Frank Adams received his PhD in Sociology from Columbia University and taught at City College in New York for two years before giving up teaching to become a pilot for TWA. However, an inflammation of the inner ear caused him to go on emergency medical leave, which he was spending in Utah. He hadn't been expecting to get back into teaching, but with nothing else to do, he called the head of the department and applied for the position.

At his interview, Dr. Adams found the department head far more interested in his experience as an airline pilot (which, back then, was considered a much sexier job) than in his teaching credentials. That suited Dr. Adams just fine. In fact, his doctoral dissertation at Columbia had been on "The Sociological Impact of Aviation on Rural Populations of North America," so he was intimately familiar with the crossover between flying and sociology.

Dr. Adams got the job and taught for the two summer semesters at a salary of $1600 per semester. The department heads were thrilled with his teaching, but didn't have any open positions, so with regret they said goodbye to Dr. Adams at summer's end, wishing him luck with his return to the skies. But Dr. Adams wasn't only popular with the teaching staff. He'd also been a hit with the students, at least 50 of whom sought him out to tell them how much they'd enjoyed his class.

From the University's perspective, that was the end of the story. Dr. Adams left Utah and never returned to teach again. Except it later surfaced that there was no Dr. Adams. Their summer substitute didn't have a PhD from Columbia, nor had he ever been an airline pilot. He also was neither a doctor nor a lawyer, despite having worked in each of those professions. He was a high school dropout turned conman named Frank Abagnale, whose exploits became famous in the 2002 hit *Catch Me If You Can* starring Leonardo DiCaprio.

Several factors contributed to Frank Abagnale becoming one of the most successful conmen in US history. First, he looked unusually old for his age, allowing him to pass himself off as a professional even while still a teen. Second, he never worked with other criminals, which meant police couldn't rely upon informants to track him down. Third, he was unpredictable in his behavior, jumping from one profession to the next rather than sticking to one consistent con.

What motivates a guy like Frank Abagnale to pose in so many professions? It certainly wasn't the money. He made a fortune passing bad checks, and each time he conned his way into a new profession, he increased his risk of capture. In fact, reading his autobiography, I couldn't shake the feeling that subconsciously he *wanted* to be caught, and it was that desire, alongside a thirst for adventure, that pushed him to try bolder cons as time went on.

Frank Abagnale was a true imposter. He worked as an unqualified doctor, an unqualified lawyer, and an unqualified university professor (though BYU disputes his claim to have taught there). True imposters like Frank Abagnale are extremely rare. Much less rare is Imposter Syndrome, which occurs when someone who's truly qualified views themselves as a fraud. One study estimated 70% of people suffer from Imposter Syndrome at least once.

I'm no exception. When I first started writing, I'd feel uncomfortable when someone would refer to me as an author or a novelist. "Nah, I'm just playing around," I'd say. "I'm not really much of a writer." But as I released more books and built a growing fan base, I could no longer deny I'd become an author.

Why do so many of us look at ourselves as imposters even when the world looks at us as qualified? Is it humility? Perhaps, but fear likely plays a greater role. My favorite line from the *Catch Me If You Can movie* comes early on, soon after Frank runs away from home and turns to a life of crime. We hear Leonardo DiCaprio's voice as he's writing a letter to his father. "Dear Dad, you always told me that an honest man has nothing to fear, so I'm trying my best not to be afraid."

Somehow, Frank Abagnale got over his fear of taking action despite being completely unqualified. He (and the rest of us) got extremely lucky he avoided any catastrophic disasters. In his book, also titled *Catch Me If You Can*, he details his near misses, such as when taking control of a plane while posing as a pilot and when treating a baby who couldn't breathe while posing as a doctor.

So how can the rest of us, who are not conmen, get over our fears of taking action and the perception we're frauds?

In 1999, Chris Baty decided to write a novel. It's not that he had a specific idea, but he, quote, "wanted to write novels for the same dumb reasons twenty-somethings start bands." Baty pulled down the shortest novel he had on his shelf, Aldous Huxley's *Brave New World*, and did a rough word count. Estimating its length at 50,000 words, Baty decided that should be the shortest acceptable length of a novel, and set it as his goal.

Writing a novel can be an extremely long process. The first Harry Potter book took J.K. Rowling seven years to write. My first novel took me six. But Chris Baty wasn't interested in starting a multi-year writing process. This was 1999, at the height of the dot-com boom. "Being surrounded by pet-supply websites worth more than Apple had a way of getting your sense of what was possible all out of whack," he later wrote. Despite having zero ideas for a story, he gave himself only one month to complete his first novel.

To be fair, Chris's idea of writing a novel in a month isn't unprecedented. In April 1951, Jack Kerouac famously wrote a draft of *On the Road* in only three weeks. Kerouac typed so fast and furiously he couldn't even handle the distraction of changing the paper on his typewriter and instead typed nonstop on a 120 foot scroll. But Kerouac had been playing with his story, based on his own life experiences, for years before his fingers hit those keys. Chris didn't have so much as a story idea. And his audaciousness didn't end there, for he had no intention of going through this mad process alone.

Chris recruited 20 friends to join him on his quest. Throughout the month, the group of them met in cafes after work to pump out the couple of thousand words they needed each night to reach their goals. Now before you get an image in your mind of Gertrude Stein, F. Scott Fitzgerald, and Ernest

Hemingway meeting in the cafes of Paris in the 1920s and scripting works of shocking brilliance, let me set the record straight. That's not where this story is going.

"Our combined post-elementary-school fiction output would have fit comfortably on a Post-it note," Chris wrote. But that didn't deter them. "The annals of rock 'n' roll are filled with self-taught musicians who recorded albums first and learned how to play their instruments much later." None of them cared they lacked experience; they were driven by sheer desire to become novelists.

This rag-tag group of writers gave themselves word quotas and ran challenges and races. "Anyone who hadn't reached their writing goal wasn't allowed to get drink refills or go to the bathroom until they hit the mark. It was ridiculous, screaming fun, and the levity of those early sessions infused what would have normally been a terrifying endeavor—writing a book in an absurdly short amount of time—into a raucous field trip to Novel-land."

The initial enthusiasm didn't last. To hit the goal without losing their day jobs, the group had to dedicate virtually all their free time to writing. Perhaps the thrill of producing great works of literature would have been enough to carry them through, but the ugly truth was, "Our novels were bad. Maybe even horrible." Half the group dropped out the second week. Those who stayed in mostly did so to save face after bragging about their plans to have a novel by the end of the month.

That came close to being the end of the story. There's only so hard we can push ourselves toward crazy goals when they offer no compelling reward. Fortunately, "The listlessness of Week Two lifted, and the flat lines of our novels began to resemble the trajectories of honest-to-G'd story arcs." And it wasn't just the story arcs that changed. "The aimless, anemic characters we'd invented in the first fourteen days began to perk up and *do* things. Quirky, unexpected, readable things...It was as if our protagonists, tired of waiting for competent stage direction from us, simply took control of the show."

On July 29th, the first participant crossed the 50,000 word finish line. Out of the twenty-one that started the challenge, six finished by the end of the month. "Everyone who participated in the escapade, though, came away from the experience changed by it." For some, that change was just the realization they never wanted to write another book again. Others fell in love with the craft and took a huge step forward as novelists.

"For me," Chris wrote, "the revelation I couldn't shake was this: The biggest thing separating people from their artistic ambitions is not a lack of talent. It's the lack of a deadline. Give someone an enormous task, a supportive community, and a friendly-yet-firm due date, and miracles will happen every time."

Far from being discouraged by the results, Chris realized he'd stumbled upon something big. As he writes in his book, *No Plot? No Problem! A Low-Stress, High-Velocity Guide to Writing a Novel in 30 Days,* "Thanks to the go-go structure of the event, the pressure to write brilliant prose had been lifted. And in its place was the pleasure of learning by doing. Of taking risks, of making messes... Writing for quantity rather than quality, I discovered, had the strange effect of bringing about both...The roar of adrenaline drowned out the self-critical voices that tend to make creative play such work for adults."

The following year, Chris moved his contest to November "to more fully take advantage of the miserable weather." His recruitment jumped to 140 participants, 21 of whom reached the 50,000 word finish line.

Chris eventually branded his initiative NaNoWriMo, short for National Novel Writing Month. By 2007, 100,000 people signed up to be Wrimos (as participants are now called) and over 15,000 of them completed 50,000 word books. A decade later, the number of Wrimos surpassed 400,000.

I joined NaNoWriMo for the first time in 2014, immediately after the publication of my first book, *The Lamp of Darkness*. I was eager to make headway on the sequel, *The Key of Rain*, and I knew my first drafts work best when I write without editing myself. This is sometimes referred to as a "vomit draft."

Each day after I wrote, I entered my word count into my profile page on NaNoWriMo, and it told me whether I was on track to become a NaNoWriMo Winner. To win, all you have to do is hit the 50,000 word goal. As Chris says, NaNoWriMo isn't about quality as much as quantity.

So how did my first NaNoWriMo experience turn out? By November 30, 2014, my novel still wasn't good, but I hit the 50,000 word goal and received a badge showing I was a winner! It took me almost four years to finish crafting *The Key of Rain* into a novel I could be truly proud of, but there was no question the NaNoWriMo platform, with its software, checkins, badges, and prizes was great fuel for getting the work done.

There are local Wrimo support groups and meetups around the world each November. The only time I went to an in-person meetup, six of us met at a local cafe. We had time for bantering ideas, silent periods for focused writing, sprints for hitting a certain word count in a fixed time, and contests where the moderator would throw out some bizarre element and tell us we all needed to fit it into the next segment of our story (I backed out of this last one as it's extremely difficult to work an iPod into a work of Biblical fiction).

I love the NaNoWriMo example as it's a *Hurry up and Fail* machine. Let's quickly unpack a few of the elements that make it so effective:

1. **Audacious Goals**: It's easier to get fired up when there's a clear, audacious goal you're trying to reach. Writing 50,000 words in 30 days certainly qualifies as audacious.

2. **Social Proof**: You don't want your goal to feel out of reach. In the NaNoWriMo community, hundreds of thousands have already hit the 50,000 word goal. This gives you the social proof to know the goal is attainable.

3. **A Clear Deadline**: You have until November 30th at midnight to complete your novel. As Chris points out, there's tremendous motivation in a deadline.

4. **Measurable Milestones**: Each day, you receive clear feedback about your pace, so you know if you're on target to reach the goal and how much you need to adjust if you fall behind.

5. **A Supportive Community**: Doing the challenge along with hundreds of thousands of other Wrimos makes the process fun, provides accountability, and takes the pressure off. As much or as little support as you want is available within NaNoWriMo forums.

6. **Rewards**: Win NaNoWriMo and you'll get a badge you can post on social media to show friends you're a winner. You can also receive discounts from NaNoWriMo sponsors when you win, such as a 50% off coupon for Scrivener, the software I'm currently using to write this book.

Of course, NaNoWriMo is more about the experience than the end product. While Wrimos hope to grow as writers and make real headway on their books, none claim it's a recipe for creating a bestseller. But what if you're not satisfied just producing junk quickly? What if your vision is to create something substantial, such as a great company?

In the next chapter, we'll have a look at how the *Hurry up and Fail* ethos is transforming the business world, particularly amongst innovative startups.

CHAPTER 4

Fail Fast, Fail Cheap

*"Science, my lad, is made up of mistakes,
but they are mistakes which it is useful to make,
because they lead little by little to the truth."*

—Jules Verne

In 1999, Nick Swinmurn, the founder of ShoeSite.com, had what he thought was a brilliant idea but couldn't get anyone to listen. Shoe sales generated $40 billion each year in the United States, but hardly any online. Nick saw a billion dollar opportunity for a shoe website, but he faced two challenges:

1. Selling shoes requires an enormous capital investment because stores must stock each shoe in many sizes. Inventory on its own might not have been a deal killer because this was still before the dotcom bubble burst, when venture capitalists were pouring millions into even moderately good ideas.

2. Most investors thought Nick had a horrible idea. No one would buy shoes online, they claimed, because shoes are a product customers need to try on before buying.

Nick was caught in a classic Catch-22. To prove to investors that customers would buy shoes online, he needed to build a website and generate substantial sales. But to build that website and prove sales, he needed investment money to cover his inventory costs. What was he to do?

To find the answer, let's jump back in time to 1783 when Benjamin Franklin, then serving as the US Ambassador to France, played a most unusual game of chess. His opponent had a dark beard, grey eyes, wore traditional Ottoman robes and a turban, and held a long Turkish smoking pipe in his left hand. He was also made of wood.

Constructed in 1770, the Mechanical Turk was presented to the world as an automaton by Hungarian inventor Wolfgang von Kempelen. Automatons were all the rage in the 18th century. They were mechanical robots that, when wound up, could perform a range of rudimentary tasks. A cuckoo clock chirping on the hour is a classic example. But the Mechanical Turk was in a category all its own. It didn't just perform a set of predetermined tasks; it played chess against human opponents, showing the ability to *think*. In their match in Paris, the Mechanical Turk defeated Franklin, one of the greatest intellectuals in US history.

At the start of each exhibition, Von Kempelen opened the wooden cabinet under the chess board to show the audience the empty cavity and the clockwork machinery inside. Then he closed the cabinet and wound the mechanism with a key. The Turk was then ready to face off against its human challengers.

The Mechanical Turk toured Europe for 84 years under multiple owners, stunning audiences, until its eventual destruction by fire in 1854. Only then did Dr. Silas Mitchell, the son of the Mechanical Turk's final owner, reveal its secret. In an article in *Chess Monthly*, Mitchell wrote, "No secret was ever kept as the Turk's has been. Guessed at, in part, many times, no one of the several explanations in our possession has ever practically solved this amusing puzzle."

The Mechanical Turk was not, as many at the time believed, a machine capable of out-thinking a human opponent. And to his credit, Von Kempelen himself never claimed it was, presenting it only as an elaborate illusion. Showing working gears inside the cabinet, winding the Turk, and other effects, including a machine that generated a clockwork sound when the Turk moved, simply helped maintain the illusion. In actuality, the cabinet had a secret compartment where a chess master could both observe the moves on the board and operate a series of levers to make the Turk respond.

The story of the Mechanical Turk probably would have remained a mostly forgotten historical footnote had it not been for Jeff Bezos and Amazon. In November 2005, the e-commerce giant launched a new service of their own called Mechanical Turk, or MTurk for short. Amazon described its new service as *artificial artificial intelligence*. Amazon's Mechanical Turk is a distributed labor tool that involves crowdsourcing workers (known as Turkers) to perform *Human Intelligence Tasks* (known as HITs) in a way that feels, as with the original Mechanical Turk, almost machinelike. A typical HIT might involve auditing user-uploaded content to make sure it's appropriate, classifying objects in satellite imagery, or converting unstructured data into standardized forms.

Fail Fast, Fail Cheap

In 2006, artist Aaron Koblin toyed with the platform and had it generate something distinctly human. He created an online drawing tool and had Turkers use it to "draw a sheep facing left." Koblin collected 10,000 sheep this way, paying a mere $0.02 per sheep. But he didn't just want the sheep at the end, he also wanted to watch the Turkers creating their sheep, to see the creative process in action. Turkers, on average, took 105 seconds to draw their sheep, meaning they only earned an average wage of $0.69 per hour. Koblin turned his sheep into a website, an exhibit, and a collection of stamps. Not bad for $200 in Turkers' fees.

Other uses of MTurk feel far more mechanical.

Business cards have been around for hundreds of years. The Chinese first started using calling cards as early as the 15th century, and precursors to the modern business card existed as early as the 17th century. The cards are still in use today, even though our shift to digital communication has made the paper cards as much a nuisance as anything else.

This was the challenge the founders of CardMunch attempted to tackle in 2009. They envisioned an app whereby iPhone users could scan business cards with their phone cameras and digitize them. The problem was Optical Character Recognition (OCR) technology was not yet strong enough to interpret the range of fonts and designs used on business cards. The CardMunch team could have waited a couple of years for the technology to catch up, but if they did, they would have lost their early-mover advantage.

So the CardMunch team got creative. Users scanned business cards into their phones, and a bit later, the system sent them a notification that their cards were digitized. Most users no doubt assumed CardMunch had developed cutting-edge OCR technology that was highly effective if a little slow. In reality, the images went to MTurk where real humans read the cards and transcribed the data. Does this business model strike you as hugely inefficient? It was, but it didn't matter.

The CardMunch model is known in business circles as a Wizard of Oz paradigm, a term coined by J.F. Kelly 30 years before the CardMunch launch. Just as the Wizard of Oz remained hidden behind a screen, pulling levers and appearing to be far more powerful than he was, the Turkers played the role of a highly advanced technology that didn't exist.

Had CardMunch planned to use human power long term, investors would have balked at the inefficiency of the business model. But CardMunch only needed human capability to prove market interest, showcase their concept, and serve as a stopgap until OCR technology improved. The Turkers provided a cheap, fast way to get a giant jump on competition. A couple of years after launch, LinkedIn bought CardMunch for $2.4 million. Two years later, LinkedIn switched to an OCR model once the technology caught up.

The Wizard of Oz paradigm allows you to test your ideas efficiently without users ever knowing you're cutting corners.

Let us return to our story of Nick Swinmurn and ShoeSite.com. Nick badly needed a Wizard of Oz solution that would give ShoeSite.com the appearance of a million dollar inventory without requiring him to have the million dollars. Nick didn't need to make profit on these initial sales, just answer the all-important question: will customers buy shoes online?

To prove his concept, Nick opened ShoeSite.com without purchasing a single pair of shoes. Instead, he went to the local mall and asked shoe retailers if they'd allow him to take pictures of *their* shoes and post them online. Since he wasn't out for short-term profit, he could fulfill these orders (if any actually came in) by going back to the stores, purchasing their shoes at retail, and shipping them out to his buyers. Yes, he'd lose money on each sale, but it was a small cost to prove whether he had a viable business model. It was worth spending a few thousand dollars to potentially procure millions from investors.

It didn't take long to receive enough sales to prove Nick's concept. A short friends-and-family funding round soon gave way to venture capital money. Normally, venture capital investors fund the existing leadership team and relegate themselves to an advisory role. Here, the venture capital investor and Nick agreed to a role reversal. Thus, investor Tony Hsieh took over Nick's role as CEO of the rebranded Zappos. A decade later, Amazon acquired Zappos for $1.2 billion.

The Wizard of Oz paradigm is one of three models we'll explore under the larger umbrella of Minimum Viable Products (MVP). In recent years, the venture capital world has become obsessed with MVPs. When funding startups, investors no longer want to dump tons of money into creating a complete product with a full range of bells and whistles before releasing it to the marketplace. Rather, they want to quickly set a product loose for public feedback. The new gadget or service still needs to function — they don't want to release buggy software — but it doesn't need to be comprehensive.

As we saw with ShoeSite.com, the MVP doesn't need to be profitable, sustainable, or even fully functional as long as it provides sufficient insights to direct new stages of funding and development. The goal is to be fast, cheap, and effective. Minimum Viable Products are all about Hurrying up and Failing to prove a business model, secure funding, or build an audience.

Let's examine two other MVP models used to Hurry up and Fail.

Fail Fast, Fail Cheap

In 2000, Joe Gebbia was a freshman at the Rhode Island School of Design. After sitting for an 8-hour long critique, known as a crit, Joe found himself with a mighty sore butt. As his classmates stood up to leave, he noticed charcoal on the bottoms of their pants from sitting on dirty art studio surfaces. These observations led Joe to create CritBuns, portable foam seat cushions shaped like butt cheeks to keep art students comfortable and their pants clean during long crits.

As this book demonstrates, failure can often be a good thing, and it certainly was with CritBuns. Had CritBuns been even a minor success, Joe might have had slightly more cash on hand a few years later when living in San Francisco. And if he had a bit more cash, he might not have felt desperate when his landlord raised his rent by 25%. And had he not felt desperate, he might not have taken desperate actions and stumbled upon a truly gigantic breakthrough. Fortunately for Joe, CritBuns were a flop. Over fifteen years after he created them, Joe still had stock and would personally go down to his basement and ship one out every time a CritBun sale trickled in, even though by this time, Joe was a billionaire.

Let's return to Joe's rent crunch. Desperate to come up with more cash, Joe and his roommate Brian tried to capitalize on a large design conference coming to San Francisco, which left hotels booked solid. They pulled three air mattresses out of their closet and posted on the conference website that attendees could rent an air mattress close to the conference for $80 a night. They even built a quick website advertising their offering and called it Air Bed and Breakfast.

These days, the AirBNB website is a pleasure to search through. I love using the map view that allows me to drag the map around a city and zoom in or out to find accommodations in precisely the location I want. I can select dates, desired number of bedrooms, price ranges, and determine if I want shared accommodation or an entire home. I can read reviews of homes and hosts, and the system stores my credit card information, allowing for easy checkout.

Back then, the Air Bed and Breakfast website had none of those features. This wasn't a Wizard of Oz scenario where Joe and Brian magically hacked together something which looked to their customers like a fully functional, professional travel site. This was the exact opposite. It was a down and dirty, bare-bones web page that just gave the critical information. It didn't even have credit card processing. Everyone who stayed with Joe and Brian paid in cash. This type of Minimum Viable Product is sometimes called the One Painkiller method. As the name implies, the One Painkiller method doesn't try to be a complete solution. Instead, it focuses on solving one pain-point, in this case that conference attendees couldn't find enough places to stay. Pains are easy to identify, their remedies often aren't. Here, the proposed painkiller was highly speculative. Would people pay money to sleep on an air mattress at the home of complete strangers?

The first clinical trial showed promise. Joe and Brian successfully rented out all three air mattresses. But here's a note of caution for anyone creating an MVP: Make sure you have sufficient evidence to determine if your product is *actually* viable. Three guests offered Joe and Brian encouragement, but were not enough to prove anything.

They recruited a former roommate, Nate, to help program the site. At this point, they considered Air Bed and Breakfast a way to provide extra housing for large conferences. They prepared for their big launch at South by Southwest, which occurs each year in Austin, Texas. This second test was a bust. Rather than scaling up from their initial experiment, all their efforts to target South by Southwest resulted in only two bookings, seriously challenging whether their idea could succeed.

The AirBNB story now takes a bizarre left turn. The partners were discouraged, cash poor, and desperately seeking an idea that would bring more enthusiasm and revenue to the business. Since the site was called Air Bed and *Breakfast*, they thought to manufacture breakfast cereal for their hosts, hoping the cereals could increase their value proposition. This idea didn't last long. A quick look at the costs involved convinced them it was a horrible idea. But the roommates moved forward with a slightly modified version: making proprietary cereal boxes and filling them with existing cereals. Specifically, with the presidential elections coming up, they created limited edition boxes of *Obama O's* and *Cap'n McCains*.

Shockingly, these political cereal boxes were a huge success. They won the struggling team national press coverage, which yielded a strong showing at that year's Democratic Convention in Denver. The cereal boxes also helped in another respect. The AirBNB crew hoped to get accepted at Y Combinator, the premier venture capital incubator. The heads of Y Combinator didn't think the idea of renting out accommodation in stranger's houses was a good one, believing people were too fearful to make it work. However, as an early stage incubator, they've learned to put more stock in entrepreneurs than in their specific business ideas because strong entrepreneurs can always pivot to stronger business models. Despite not liking the AirBNB concept, the cereal gambit convinced Y Combinator to take a chance on AirBNB because it showed the founders had the grit and creativity they were looking for, even if their idea seemed stupid.

But even those who thought they had a ridiculous idea couldn't deny it actually made money in its initial trials. Getting a website up fast, testing it, and tweaking it allowed them to develop the powerful platform they have today. By using the One Painkiller process, the AirBNB founders proved within just a few days that at least one aspect of their business plan could work. Once upon a time, investors couldn't fathom AirBNB competing with hotels. Now, they have more rooms than the largest hotel chains in the world.

So far, we've looked at two types of MVPs: the Wizard of Oz and the One Painkiller. But not all products can be shoved into one of these modalities. Take, for instance, the development of a new car. You can't exactly Wizard of Oz the customer into buying an illusion of a car that doesn't exist. Nor can you easily create a car with just one key feature, as in the One Painkiller technique. So what do you do then?

In 2006, Drew Houston took the notorious Fung Wah bus to New York to visit friends. The Fung Wah ran between Boston's South Station and New York's Chinatown for a fraction of the cost of mainstream bus lines. A quick scan of Fung Wah reviews includes: "Cheap and frequent but crappy and potentially deadly;" "Probably the cheapest way to commit suicide. Some of their drivers don't even have a valid driver's license;" and "Expect the ride to be worse than a roller coaster."

But despite the hazardous conditions, the Fung Wah remained popular with students and others with limited funding who found the $10 to $15 ticket price a bargain. With little in his pocket after graduating from MIT, Drew preferred the cheap prices to riding on a bus line that didn't falsify its safety inspection reports.

Just as the Fung Wah pulled out of South Station, Drew had the horrible realization he'd left his thumb drive behind. Back in 2006, if you wanted to share data between your computers, the most convenient way was via a USB thumb drive. Without his drive, Drew had no way to access his data and do his intended work. He never wanted to be stuck in this situation again, and right there on the Fung Wah, he pulled out his laptop and started coding a solution to his problem.

Drew envisioned a cloud-based platform which could sync files so they'd be accessible from anywhere. That way, if he forgot his thumb drive or if it got destroyed when the Fung Wah caught fire (not as uncommon as you might think) he could still access his data with an internet connection. Also, if his laptop were stolen or even crushed the next time the Fung Wah rolled over (also happened), Drew's data would be safe and could quickly be downloaded onto his new computer.

Hurry Up and Fail

It didn't take Drew long to develop a working prototype. The problem was, his business model was resource heavy. He wanted to create off-site storage for the internet, which would require tremendous server space. And it wasn't just space he needed. His premise was based on keeping user data safe, meaning his system needed to have exceptional security and stability. So while building a prototype for one person for testing purposes was quick and inexpensive, scaling the business to service millions would cost a fortune.

Drew knew his best bet was to procure serious venture capital funding. Just like Joe Gebbia and AirBNB, he set his sights on Y Combinator. A friend there got him in front of Paul Graham, the managing director, and Drew showed up with his laptop and tried to demo the product for Paul. Big mistake. Paul threw Drew out on his ear without looking at the demo. He said the whole reason they had an application process was so they wouldn't have people showing up off the street trying to pitch them.

Now Drew was in a tough spot. A day earlier, he'd been a nobody to Paul Graham. Suddenly, he was worse than a nobody. He was on Paul's blacklist. Drew needed to reverse his fortunes. He wanted to get Pau's attention and convince him he was a guy worth dealing with. But how?

So far, we've explored two models of the Minimum Viable Product, but neither of those was a good fit. Drew couldn't launch his product using the Wizard of Oz paradigm. He needed to *actually* save users' data securely, not just *appear* to. The One Painkiller technique was also a no-go. Unlike AirBNB, which launched with an extremely basic website created in just a few days, Drew's product required elaborate and expensive server infrastructure to go live with even its most basic features.

After being run out of Paul's office in disgrace, Drew realized venture capitalists like Paul spent much of their day following Hacker News and other sites reporting on the latest in technology. If he could create enough buzz on Hacker News, he might restore his dignity and get the Y Combinator team chasing after him. He didn't actually need any users to try out his product, he just needed enough people to understand and get excited about his concept.

Next to the Wizard of Oz paradigm and the One Painkiller technique, Drew's chosen method seems incredibly simple. For his MVP, he simply created a video demonstration of his product, which he'd titled Dropbox. This video was nothing more than a screen capture of Drew using Dropbox on his computer, accompanied by Drew's voiceover walking the viewer through its functionality.

The result?

The tech world went nuts. Drew's video shot up to the top spot on Hacker News and stayed there for days. No one had ever seen a service quite like

Fail Fast, Fail Cheap

Dropbox before. Many wanted to sign up on the spot, but they couldn't, as the service didn't yet exist. Instead, viewers were taken to a page where they could leave their email to join the waitlist for early access to Dropbox.

Dropbox shot from a complete unknown to a tool techies drooled over but couldn't get. Within 48 hours, everyone who mattered in Silicon Valley venture capital firms had Dropbox on their radar, including Paul Graham. The long email list of those who signed up for an early shot at Dropbox proved a tremendous market demand. That demand got Drew into Y Combinator and secured the funding he needed to launch. The huge waitlist allowed him to grow the service gradually, giving access to just as many users as he could handle for each stage of development.

Some might think Drew's explainer video wasn't an MPV at all since it didn't involve a product release. But remember, the point of an MVP is not sales or profitability; it's feedback. Drew's explainer video conveyed to potential customers exactly what his product would do. Viewer response could have been critical or, worse, silent. Such results would have sent him back to the drawing board to make tweaks and try again. Instead, he received a clear message he was on track.

Elon Musk used this same technique on November 22, 2019, when he announced the release of the new Tesla Cybertruck. If you haven't seen the Cybertruck, it's a pickup shaped like a chrome and glass pyramid that belongs in a sci-fi movie.

To show the hardness of its stainless steel alloy exterior, Musk pounded the Cybertruck with a sledgehammer, which didn't leave a mark. Then an assistant threw a metal ball at the windows to show the strength of the "armor glass." This time, the live demo was a failure, and the glass cracked. But as we've learned throughout this book, failures aren't always the disasters they seem. In fact, the cracked window gave the Cybertruck live demo so much publicity that some speculated Musk did it on purpose (since Musk swore on stage when the window cracked, I don't think it was intentional).

Still, Musk laughed off the failure and kept going with the demo. He wowed the audience with the truck's speed: going from 0 to 60 in only 2.9 seconds; its range: up to 500 miles on a single charge; and its price: coming in at under $40,000 for the base model.

Of course, the real test of the demo wasn't whether the glass broke, but how many people would put their money where their mouth was. The day of the demo, 146,000 people made a deposit to pre-order a Cybertruck.

The incredible thing about the Cybertruck demo was that Tesla didn't intend to kick off production until the end of 2021, a full two years later. But the demo proved a healthy market for the product, created tons of buzz, raised tens of millions of dollars in paid deposits, and boosted the stock price.

Hurry Up and Fail

The point of this chapter is not to detail all varieties of Minimum Viable Products. A quick online search will reveal more variations. The point is to show the power of quickly and inexpensively putting your ideas out to generate genuine feedback and a way forward.

Imagine for a moment Joe Gebbia and his partners had created and stuck to a five year plan for AirBNB. Had they kept their heads above water, they would have wound up with a business offering air mattresses to conference attendees rather than becoming the world's largest hotelier. Their success came from making iteration after iteration, each time seeing what was working and what wasn't, and adapting to the feedback of their hosts and customers.

The MVP ideology is all about speeding up the feedback loop. Don't spend two years constructing a great vacation rental website when you can hack together a basic website in three days that will still solve your customers' number one pain point. The initial AirBNB website didn't need to accept credit cards or have a map view in order to answer their primary question: Would people pay to stay at a stranger's apartment?

For AirBNB, the One Painkiller technique gave them fast, concrete feedback. Zappos used the smoke and mirrors of the Wizard of Oz paradigm, and Dropbox made a quick and dirty product demo. All three companies received feedback in a matter of days that could have taken years had they used the more traditional route of waiting for a fully functional product to launch.

Do you also have a product or idea you're excited to release to the world? Which Minimum Viable Product techniques can speed up your feedback loop? Here are a few things to consider when designing your MVP.

1. **Identify your target market.** Who exactly is your MVP meant to serve?

2. **Define the core problem your MVP will solve.** An MVP shouldn't be everything to everyone. Focus on one core issue.

3. **Select the key features.** Avoid adding any extra features that aren't critical to your MVP.

4. **Set clear objectives.** This is what your MVP is trying to prove or disprove. Will people buy shoes online? Will people pay money to stay in someone else's home?

5. **Collect feedback.** How will you know if your idea is a good one or not? What does success look like? Feedback is essential and later in the book, we'll examine ways to effectively gather and evaluate it.

6. **Iterate quickly.** You may not get a clear 'yes' or 'no' on your first try. Use the feedback to make improvements and keep putting out new versions.

7. **Keep costs low.** Remember, an MVP should be a low-cost test of your idea.

But what if you just don't feel ready to put your idea out into the world because you're afraid the public will reject it? If fear is blocking you from moving forward, I have news for you. You're not alone.

CHAPTER 5

Learn to Love Rejection

"There is only one thing that makes a dream impossible to achieve: the fear of failure."

- PAULO COELHO

If the Feds caught Roger counterfeiting one more time, they were going to lock him up and throw away the key. But Roger was a counterfeiter to the bone and wasn't about to give it up for a legitimate job. He just needed a better strategy, one that wouldn't raise the ire of the Treasury Department.

This was in the late 1950s, well before frequent flyer miles and cash back credit cards. Back then, there was one giant customer rewards program that dwarfed all others: S&H Green Stamps. At its peak, S&H claims it was printing 3 times as many stamps as the US Postal Service, and 80% of households collected them. You could buy nearly anything with their Green Stamps: appliances, cars, vacations, even a pair of gorillas (the gorillas were donated to zoos).

Unlike dollars, which were difficult to copy, Roger realized the Green Stamps were moronically simple. He could make counterfeits indistinguishable from the real thing. And these stamps weren't under the jurisdiction of the feared Treasury Department. In no time, Roger could print millions of them, and anything in the S&H catalog could be his.

There was only one problem. The glue Roger used wouldn't work in his licking machine, and he had to lick each stamp to put it into the redemption books. Picture this: Roger the counterfeiter becomes a victim of his own success, making himself sick and slowly withering away as he licks and pastes stamp after stamp in his redemption books. Meanwhile, his mother is negotiating with S&H on how many books of stamps they'd need to redeem for a new house in the suburbs. A tempting reward for her, a potential death sentence for him.

If the above storyline reminds you of the warped plots of Stephen King, that's because it is. A very young Stephen King. While not the first story he ever submitted for publication, this was the first he considered a strong, original idea. He wrote up *Happy Stamps* and submitted it to *Alfred Hitchcock's Mystery Magazine*. Three weeks later, the story came back with a rejection slip. At the bottom of the slip was a handwritten note telling him not to staple his submissions in the future. That's all the feedback he received, not a word on the rejected story.

Plenty of young writers have submitted stories to magazines and received similar rejection slips. In fact, while taking a creative writing course in college, one of my professors insisted we all submit stories for publication just so we could know what it felt like to receive a rejection letter. When we asked him about what would happen if our stories were accepted, he assured us we had nothing to worry about. None of us yet had the skill to be published.

The rejection letter I received in that class was the last I received for years. Not because I was so good, but because I stopped writing when the class ended. I in no way thought my writing was good enough to have a future as a writer, and the rejection letter proved I was right.

I wonder how many thousands of young writers submit exactly one story for publication their entire lives? They then await the publisher's verdict: do they have the skill to be *real* writers or are they just pretending? When their first rejection letter inevitably comes in, the little voice in the back of their heads has all the confirmation it needs. They'd tried, they'd failed. It was time to give up writing and apply for law school.

But when Stephen King got his rejection letter for *Happy Stamps*, he didn't conclude the publishing world had deemed him forever unworthy. Instead, he pounded a nail into the wall above his Webcor phonograph, wrote "*Happy Stamps*" on the rejection slip, then poked it onto the nail. He recalls in his book *On Writing*, "I felt pretty good, actually. When you're still too young to shave, optimism is a perfectly legitimate response to failure."

King's rejection nail didn't last long. Not because he was so good no one turned him down. As he recounts, "By the time I turned fourteen (and shaving twice a week, whether I needed to or not) the nail in my wall would no longer support the weight of the rejection slips impaled upon it. I replaced the nail with a spike and went on writing."

Learn to Love Rejection

There are times I'll read passages in Stephen King's *11/22/63* (one of my all time favorite books) and just shake my head, wishing I could write like that. I remind myself King wasn't born with a genius for description or character development. He pumped out enough stories by age fourteen that the rejection slips alone overwhelmed a nail. Not only did he Hurry Up and Fail, he shifted rejection from a negative to a positive, to something that could propel him to work harder rather than drag him down.

As we saw in Part 1, when we view trial and failure as a positive rather than a negative, we open the floodgates to learning and growth. But there's a subset of failure that most of us find particularly difficult to handle: rejection. I might try my hand at baking a cake and if it comes out lousy, I can just dump it in the trash and move on. But with rejection, I'm no longer the judge of my worthiness. I pass that power on to another. And most of us hate to be judged, largely out of fear that we'll be rejected.

Stephen King moved toward rejection rather than shunning it, and as a result, he accelerated his growth as a writer. How is your ability to handle rejection? Could you imagine getting rejection after rejection and keep moving forward with the same optimism and determination?

If your answer is no, beware. It's going to cost you.

Women, on average, earn 81 percent of what men make in the United States. Some look at this number and conclude there's clear gender discrimination in the workplace. Others say, 'not so fast,' and point out that most of the gap can be explained by career choice, as fewer women want to work high-intensity, high-pay, 60-hour-a-week jobs. Many women intentionally choose lower paying careers that provide greater work/life balance.

So can career choices alone explain the gender wage gap? Not entirely, no. There is another aspect of the pay gap that is rarely discussed in the debate and has nothing to do with differing career paths.

In 2020, I interviewed Bernadette Joy as part of a virtual summit I ran called *Financial Independence School*. Bernadette (who I always think of as Burn-a-Debt) has spent over a decade in HR and now runs *Crush Your Money Goals*, helping women pay off debt and get ahead financially. She explained another aspect of the wage gap I'd never considered.

"During my time in HR, I'd say the majority of men I made job offers to made a counteroffer asking for more money. But most of the women I made offers to took it right away. I can probably count on one hand the number of women who negotiated."

Personally, I'd never worked in corporate America and I knew little about pay structures or how salaries were determined. So I asked, "Can you give me an example of a man who successfully negotiated?"

"Sure," she said. "I remember one guy. He was just coming out of college. We made him an offer for $80,000 a year, which I thought was a ton. He told me he wanted $140,000. I thought he was crazy, but I told him I'd pass along the request to my manager. The manager said, 'we'll meet him at $120,000,' and my jaw hit the floor."

"So he got 50% more just for asking for it?"

"Yep."

But surely there must be risks to negotiating, right? I asked Bernadette, "In all your years in HR, did you ever rescind a job offer because someone negotiated?"

"No."

"And what percent of the time did those who negotiate end up making more?"

"The majority of the time they wound up making more."

Stop and think about that for a moment. Here is an HR veteran telling us negotiating had tremendous upside and absolutely no financial downside. And yet, the vast majority of women didn't do it. Why? Culprit number one is the paralyzing fear of rejection. If we don't ask, we won't have to suffer the indignity of being turned down.

Hear this now: Those who can't handle rejection settle for less. If you can't ask for more money, you might get paid less than another doing the exact same job. If you can't handle asking someone on a date, you might have to settle for less love in your life. If you can't ask for a promotion, you may have to settle for advancing at a slower rate than others with less talent.

To further illustrate, here's a quick snippet from *The Size of Your Dreams*, a novel my wife and I wrote to teach readers techniques for achieving their goals.

> *"What separates great salespeople from ordinary ones?" Mr. Griffin asked.*
>
> *Christy shrugged. "I suppose it's the ability to get people to say yes."*
>
> *"That's the second greatest distinction. More important is the ability to hear the word no."*
>
> *"How does that help?" Jarod asked.*
>
> *"Ordinary salespeople go out on a sales call, and if they get a no, they get discouraged. The great ones hear no after no and keep going. Some even tell themselves that they need to hear no ten times to get one yes. Getting a no actually excites*

Learn to Love Rejection

them, as they tell themselves that it brings them closer and closer to getting a yes."

Rejection is like a muscle. A person who lifts a 50 pound weight once in their life might be sore for days afterwards. But someone who pumps iron every day won't even notice it. Stephen King had to move from a nail to a spike to hold his rejection slips, but he plugged away and became one of the bestselling authors in history.

So I want to ask you again: where do you stack up in terms of rejection? Are you someone who has no problem asking for what you want? If you get rejected, can you just shrug it off and move on?

If you're like most people, my guess is you don't always feel comfortable asking for what you want. Even worse, when you do ask and get rejected, I bet it stings with humiliation and shame. The question is, can you live with momentary discomfort if it's the key to getting what you want in life?

What if I told you it was possible to reduce or even eliminate that discomfort, so it never gets in your way?

Jia Jiang was six years old when his teacher decided to encourage her elementary school students to give compliments to their classmates. One by one, the students received praise from their peers, but none of them volunteered any compliments about Jia. The humiliation he felt that day would haunt him for decades.

Twenty-four years later, Jia still couldn't shake the fear of rejection he traced back to that early childhood event. At this point, he was married, with a child on the way, and had left his high-paying job to build his own startup. But that old fear threatened to sink the fledgling business. He'd only gotten up the nerve to approach a single investor to back his startup, and when the investor said no, he was ready to quit.

But his wife wasn't ready to let him give up just yet. "I gave you six months, I didn't give you four," she said to him, referring to their agreement that he could take six months without a job to try starting his own business. "You have two months left. Keep going and leave no regret!"

So there Jia found himself, with two months to secure an investor, but with a debilitating fear of rejection blocking him from reaching out. To save his business, Jia realized he needed to stop running from rejection and start co-existing with it.

His online search for how to overcome rejection eventually led Jia to *Rejection Therapy*, a card game created by Canadian entrepreneur Jason Comely. The game is simple: you pick a card and must do whatever it says. One card requires you to walk up to a stranger and convince them you know them. Another has you submit a pitch to *Dragon's Den* (the Canadian version of *Shark Tank*). Each task is designed to make you face rejection. Comely's claim was that once you seek out rejection, you'll find it's not as bad as you feared. By repeating this process over and over, the fear of rejection dissipates.

Jia loved the *Rejection Therapy* idea. "Maybe I've seen too many kung fu movies," he writes in his book, *Rejection Proof*, "but the idea of overcoming rejection by throwing myself at it again and again and again held an odd sort of appeal." Jia took the concept one step further and committed himself to face rejection 100 days in a row. Not only would he put himself in circumstances where he was likely to be told "no," but he'd further confront his fear by videoing the rejections and posting them on a blog tracking his progress.

The first day, he walked up to the security guard in his building and asked to borrow $100. The guard rejected him, as Jia knew he would, but also asked him why he needed the money. Jia was too stressed at the rejection to answer, but later that evening, as he was posting the video, he reflected on the guard's question. If he had a compelling answer and gave the guard reason to trust him, would the guard have reconsidered? Jia realized the way he posed his requests could impact his results.

On day 2, he went to Five Guys for lunch and ordered a bacon cheeseburger. He noticed the soda machine had a sign offering free refills, but he didn't want more soda; he wanted another burger. So for his rejection of the day, Jia approached the counter and asked for a burger refill. When the guy said no, Jia asked why they offered refills on soda but not on burgers? The guy told him that's just the way it is, but he chuckled when he said it. Already Jia was starting to see there wasn't so much to fear in these rejections.

On day 3, Jia walked into Krispy Kreme and asked for five donuts interlinked in the shape of Olympic rings. The woman asked him when he'd like them. The question caught him off-guard. After all, his goal had been to get rejected. Not knowing what else to do, he said he needed them in fifteen minutes. The woman pulled out a piece of paper and drew out the rings to make sure she had the idea right, then said, "Let me see what I can do."

Fifteen minutes later, a shocked Jia walked out with a box full of donuts arranged like Olympic rings. He hadn't realized at the time how much getting that surprise "yes" would change his life. He posted the video online, like he had the previous two days. Except this time, it took off like wildfire. Jia's video of Jackie, the Krispy Kreme lady, making him Olympic ring donuts received millions of views. In a matter of days, he went from being an ordinary guy trying to get through his own fear of rejection, to becoming a celebrity rejection expert. Talk shows called to interview him about his rejection journey. He was pitched on hosting a reality TV show as the Rejection Whisperer. He flew around the country giving talks on rejection.

Before his 100 days of rejection were up, he'd achieved so much success on his rejection journey that he closed his startup to teach about rejection full time.

A few years ago, I learned firsthand the power of putting aside my fear of rejection and asking for more. Over the course of two days, I called all my vendors in my core business, cabinet hardware sales, with a long list of questions and requests. I asked each vendor what margins their best customer received. I expected the vendors to tell me this was proprietary information, but virtually all of them were happy to share their numbers. If they had customers receiving better pricing, I next asked what I'd have to do to get the same margins. Some of them improved my pricing on the spot, just because I'd asked! Others told me they had criteria I had to meet, such as purchasing a minimum number of display boards, placing a large inventory order, or increasing my sales volume.

I asked if I could get better shipping rates. I asked if they'd be willing to cover any of my advertising expenses (known in the industry as co-op advertising). I'd estimate the calls took no more than six hours total. Most of them didn't lead to increased margins. But enough of them yielded fruit that I increased profits by thousands of dollars a year. Had I called a decade earlier, my additional profits would have been in the tens, if not hundreds, of thousands of dollars.

At first, I felt like an idiot for waiting so long to make these calls. But the more conversations I had, the more I got the impression my requests were anything but ordinary. When I asked one vendor about co-op advertising money, the response I received was, "No one's ever asked for that before. Let me ask my manager and I'll get back to you." A week later, she replied with a "yes." I know this brand deals with thousands of customers, yet shockingly, none of them thought to ask.

Most importantly, I didn't damage a single relationship by reaching out. At worst, I received a polite "no" in response to my requests, but I didn't lose any vendors or create bad blood.

Remember, failing to ask is asking to fail. If you can move toward rejection rather than shrink from it, it will open a whole new world of options. Take a moment to consider the following questions:

1. **What steps can you take to build your resilience in the face of rejection?** Can you take a page from Jia Jiang and put yourself in positions to face rejection more often rather than less?

2. **What requests can you make *right now* that you've been avoiding?**

3. **Who's effort, wisdom, or money could you recruit to move your goals forward?**

4. **Think about the biggest failures you've faced.** In retrospect, was there someone you could have turned to for help but didn't?

5. **The next time you find yourself afraid to make a big ask, pause and reflect on the possible outcomes.** How much will you gain if you get a 'yes'? What will it cost you if you get a 'no'? You might find the potential gains hugely outweigh the losses.

Nothing in this book will make you immune to rejection, but as we'll see in the next chapter, there are steps we can take to reduce the impact of being rejected.

CHAPTER 6

Fail Small, Fail Often

"Failures are the stairs we climb to reach success."

—Roy T. Bennett

Jordan Harbinger spent 11 years building his podcast audience, his email list, and his social media following. He lost them all overnight. These listeners downloaded his show, *The Art of Charm*, an average 4.1 million times per month. But a split with his partners at *The Art of Charm* led Jordan to walk away, and he didn't do it alone. Most of the production staff exited with him. All of which left Jordan with a gigantic problem: how was he supposed to support a sizable staff, let alone himself, when he had zero subscribers?

Fortunately, Jordan had two things going for him. First, he was no stranger to extricating himself from tight situations. This is a man who'd been kidnapped and escaped. Not once, but twice. Besides having the internal strength to get himself out of tight jams, Jordan had an external asset as well. It's this second asset that will help us understand the focus of this chapter: the immense cumulative power of frequent, low-stakes actions.

When I think of radio personalities, I picture larger than life, highly extroverted individuals. But when growing up, Jordan hated attention. "Now they call it social anxiety, but then it was just you're a big weirdo."

Jordan's social anxieties drove him to frequently skip school, and even though he made it through college, he graduated without a clear passion or career path. "I did what a lot of guys do when they run out of career options, and I became an attorney."

Let's take a moment to discuss how corporate law firms work. Attorneys track their time meticulously to bill for minutes spent working for a specific client. Any time spent on lunch breaks, bathroom visits, chatting with coworkers, networking events, skill development, etc., doesn't count as billable hours, the single most important metric to the corporate lawyer. Big New York firms expect their attorneys to bill at least 2000 hours per year, and given how much time non-billable activities take, this can lead to an extremely long workweek.

The shy newbie had no problem working late into the night, pouring over legal documents to clock his time. But one aspect of his first few months in corporate law didn't go so well. All new associates were supposed to have a mentor in the firm, but Jordan's mentor kept blowing him off. While most attorneys barely saw the light of day, Jordan's mentor, on the rare occasions he was spotted in the firm, always had a tan. He spent more time traveling and playing golf than poring through case law.

The other associates in the firm were going out to Blue Man Group and the finest restaurants with their mentors, while Jordan's wouldn't even speak to him. Finally, HR put enough pressure on the mentor that he agreed to a short meeting at the Starbucks in the lobby. Even then, Jordan didn't get his mentor's full attention — he kept checking messages on his Blackberry — but at least he said, "OK, ask me anything you want."

Jordan asked him, "How come you're never in the office but you're a partner and you make a lot of money?"

"Mostly, I generate business for the firm."

That response made no sense to Jordan. Where were this guy's billable hours?

The mentor explained he had friends at several big investment banks, and if his friends were out biking, golfing, or playing squash, he joined them because his value to the firm outside the office was greater than his value inside the office. He didn't worry about missing his billable hour bonus each year because he received commissions on the deals he brought in.

Until then, Jordan knew of two ways to get ahead in law: outworking and outsmarting his peers. His mentor presented a third way, a way that required neither crazy hours nor legal expertise. It was the power of building a strong network and leveraging it. The mentor emphasized the ability to bring in business was hugely valuable, and if Jordan could excel in this area, it could be a strong path to success.

Just what every introvert with social anxiety loves to hear.

I also know a thing or two about a social anxiety blocking a clear pathway to success. As I mentioned in the introduction, the first time Chana and I attempted to build a course around our book *The Size of Your Dreams*, we discarded the videos we shot in Ecuador, never even reviewing them. In that version, only Chana appeared on camera while I worked behind the scenes. Why? Because I was terrified of being filmed.

Fail Small, Fail Often

Ironically, an unrelated event in that same rainforest forced me to face my fear of the camera. I was taking an online course with Russell Brunson, one of my favorite marketers, when he made a bold claim. "If you publish every day for a year, I promise it will change your life." Publishing, he explained, could take one of three forms: a blog post, a podcast episode, or a video. He advised playing to strengths. "If you're a good writer, then blog. If you have a good voice, podcast. If you're good on camera, video."

I thought about his claim all day. I'd already published three novels, so I could clearly write. I'd never loved blogging, but with the promise it would change my life, what did I have to lose? I committed to a year of daily blog posts.

That commitment only lasted a few hours. In the evening, Russel's right-hand man, Stevie Boom-Boom, did a live session to clarify and reinforce the Russel's lessons from earlier in the day (Stevie Boom-Boom's real name is Stephen Larson, though he quickly earned the Boom-Boom nickname in our family for the earsplitting "Boom" he screamed into the mic at the beginning of each class). Boom-Boom agreed everyone in the course absolutely had to start publishing immediately, but he gave slightly different advice than his mentor. Boom-Boom said if we liked reading blog posts we should blog, if we liked listening to podcasts we should podcast, and if we liked watching videos we should make videos.

This may sound like a small difference, but to me it was huge. Whereas Russel advised me to go after my area of greatest skill, Boom-Boom advised me to go after my area of greatest passion. Even though I was a writer, I never had the slightest interest in reading blog posts. But I loved watching videos. Unfortunately, as I mentioned above, I was deathly afraid of the camera. Even at our wedding, I refused to have a videographer because I knew I'd freeze up.

It would have been easy to ignore Boom-Boom's advice. After all, he was contradicting the counsel of his own mentor, one of the world's top marketers. But in my gut I knew Boom-Boom was right. If I got on camera every day for a year, if I faced my fear every single day, that would transform my life. I resolved to do it. I would make a daily video.

But I didn't.

Days passed and no filming took place. My fear of getting on camera loomed too large.

Despite my hesitation to make videos, this 30-day challenge was the best and cheapest marketing course I'd ever taken, so I enrolled again the next time it ran (course details are in the notes section at the end). Since I learn best when teaching, I recruited a dozen friends to take the course with me. Each week we met as a group, and I added whatever insights I'd learned since my first time through. When we got back to the section about publishing every day, I knew I couldn't encourage my peers to do it if I wasn't going to follow through myself.

Russell always said it's no big deal going on camera. When you start out, you'll most likely only have your mom watching anyway. So on my 45th birthday, I decided to record myself and publicly commit to publishing at least 250 videos by the time I reached 46.

I set up my phone and got ready to record. I stared at the camera. The camera's electric eye stared back at me. I froze up again. I so needed to get over my fear. The problem was, I always thought I looked ridiculous on camera. And how many thousands of times had I said aloud that I *hated* being on camera?

As we saw in the section about Sara Blakely and her father, the words we use and the stories we tell have tremendous power. I needed a new story, and I needed it fast, as the day was coming to a close. Fortunately, I knew a thing or two about the dynamics of changing beliefs. I jumped up and down until I got myself into a high energy state and screamed out, "I love the camera! The camera loves me! I love the camera! The camera loves me!"

I kept screaming it until I believed I wouldn't be a total loser on camera. I hit record, and the first time I stumbled over a word, I felt like a total loser on camera. I jumped again, I screamed again, I hit record again, I stumbled again, I felt like a loser again. Rinse and repeat, rinse and repeat.

I don't recall how many times I messed up before I finally had a take I was willing to post online, but fortunately my phone didn't run out of memory. I shared it with trepidation, but of course, all I got back was positive reinforcement and birthday wishes. No one told me I was deluding myself or I had no business posting online videos, even if they were thinking it.

Russell was wrong about one thing. He said only my mom would watch in the beginning, but even she didn't stick around long (she watched one or two videos and gave up). My videos were awful, and it wasn't just because I was awkward. I also skipped from topic to topic completely at random. Some days I'd talk about spiritual concepts, other times business tactics. I alienated most of my meager audience within a matter of days, and I'm sure quite a few of my "friends" quickly unfollowed me.

But by this point, I didn't care. I wasn't making the videos for "them" anyway. These videos were all for me, and it didn't take long to see improvements. I improved my posture, body language, and volume. I learned how to edit videos. I created intros. I tweaked my lighting and audio. Little by little, I got better.

Fifteen months later, when we launched the live version of *Dream, Design, Manifest*, I no longer questioned whether I belonged on camera. Russell promised that publishing every day would change my life, and it did. Hurrying Up and

Fail Small, Fail Often

Failing on video helped me transition from a reclusive writer who taught from behind a keyboard to an online teacher able to interact with my audience.

The key to my transformation was lowering the stakes by creating lots of low-risk opportunities to fail. Had I waited to get on camera until an enormous opportunity came along, one so big I couldn't say no despite my fear of being filmed, I would have risked catastrophic disaster. Instead, I took baby steps each day, hitting my point of discomfort over and over, until I slowly expanded my comfort zone.

The cumulative impact of many small steps can be huge, often much greater than the impact of gigantic efforts made on a less frequent basis. And this was ultimately the key to how an attorney with social anxiety overcame his fear of people and built himself a robust network.

Let's return to the story of Jordan Harbinger, who just learned that strong networking skills could be an easier and more reliable path to success than slaving at his desk late into the night.

Have you ever noticed that those who struggle most to learn a skill often become the best teachers? When one spends years of deliberate effort mastering something, they develop an understanding of its nuances that a natural might never grasp. Perhaps that's why Forbes now refers to this former introvert as one of the best relationship builders anywhere.

Jordan speaks five languages, and he'll tell you the key to learning a language is full immersion. But when it comes to networking, he teaches the opposite. To build strong networks, you don't need to fully immerse yourself into the world of the socialite. Rather, much like my experience getting over my fear of the camera, you need to take purposeful, simple actions each day. On his website, Jordan offers a free class called *6 Minute Networking*, which walks through the steps anyone can take to strengthen their network if they're willing to dedicate 6 minutes every day.

Why space out your networking over time? Because, as Jordan points out, when you're already thirsty, it's too late to dig a well.

What does that mean?

Imagine this scenario. You go into the office one day, and the boss wants to see you. She's real sorry, she says, but earnings are down and the board decided to make cuts. With no warning, you find yourself unemployed with nothing but a one month severance check to fall back on. So what do you do? You probably start brainstorming who could help. Then perhaps you send out messages saying, "Hey, long time no speak. I hope you're doing well. I was wondering, perhaps you could help me out…"

One of Jordan's exercises is to think of the first ten or fifteen people you would contact if you ever found yourself laid off and desperate. If these are the people you'd seek out in a crisis, these relationships are too important to risk fading. You want to reengage those people now while things are good and when you don't need anything. In fact, while everything is going well for you, see if there's any help you can give them. Strengthen these relationships before you need them. Dig your wells before you're thirsty.

When Jordan left *The Art of Charm*, he lost his email subscribers, his social media followers, and all of his iTunes subscribers, an audience that took him 11 years to build. Having already been the host of a successful podcast, Jordan figured it wouldn't take him 11 years to rebuild an audience, but still expected it to be a long haul, perhaps even five years, to return to his former number of listeners.

But while he didn't have subscribers, he still had his personal contacts. For years, he'd been building and nurturing his network of friends. The question was, would they respond now that he needed help? Many of us find it easier to give help than to ask for it in return. Jordan, who struggled for so many years with social anxiety, was nervous about the reaction he'd get now that he was in need. But he made the phone calls, he sent the messages, and then he waited to see results.

This is a book about failure. So did Jordan's outreach attempts fail?

No doubt many of them did. Whenever anyone engages in an outreach campaign like this one, they can expect a huge failure rate. Had Jordan banked on only one or two individuals exerting themselves on his behalf, he might have found himself at a dead end. However, because he had spent years performing small, daily networking tasks, he built relationships with so many influential individuals that the failures didn't inhibit his success.

One person he reached out to was Tom Bilyeu, host of *Impact Theory*. Tom had Jordan on his show to talk about the launch of his new podcast, *The Jordan Harbinger Show*, and during the episode, Tom described how the two of them first met. "Out of nowhere [Jordan] reaches out to me and says, 'Hey, I've been watching your show. I think it's fantastic. Let me know how I can help.' I was like 'Whoa, Jordan Harbinger just reached out to me, this is crazy.'" This initial outreach occurred when Tom was fairly new to podcasting and Jordan was already a star. Jordan had suggested guests for Tom's show, and Tom replied they tried to get those exact people but couldn't land them. Jordan stepped in and made introductions, helping Tom get the high-profile guests he wanted. Tom concluded the story by saying to Jordan, "I have said privately a thousand times…no one outside of this company has had a bigger impact on this company than you."

Tom was part of a cadre of influencers who rushed to answer Jordan's call for help. Within three weeks, the brand new *Jordan Harbinger Show* had over a million downloads. Apple recognized his podcast as the best and most downloaded new show of 2018. Two years later, his monthly downloads topped six million, about 50% higher than *The Art of Charm* reached at its peak.

When I came out with my fourth book, *The Cash Machine: A Tale of Passion, Persistence, and Financial Independence*, I knew I needed a different approach to book marketing. All three of my previous books had their loyal fans, but despite strong reviews, none of them broke through to be consistent bestsellers. In many ways, it would have been easier if I received lackluster feedback. But with the two books I'd released the year before, *The Key of Rain* and *The Size of Your Dreams*, the feedback and reviews were incredibly positive, which left me frustrated. Why? Because I knew the lack of sales was a direct reflection on my pathetic book marketing, not the quality of my books.

Podcasts struck me as a wonderful medium to spread the word about *The Cash Machine*. The podcast format gives listeners a chance to delve into the meat of a subject, and I've often picked up books myself that I first learned about on podcasts. For years, I'd dreamed about appearing on one of my favorite podcasts like *The School of Greatness* by Lewis Howes. But as I thought about a promotion plan for *The Cash Machine*, a realization hit me: I wasn't ready for the big leagues.

Getting booked on a top podcast is about more than writing a good book. Here I was, this massive introvert who had hardly given any interviews. What would happen if Lewis Howes suddenly called and invited me on his show? I'd stumble over my message, I'd get frazzled by his questions. Of course, all that was merely theoretical, because even if he somehow read and loved my book, I doubt he'd invite me if I hadn't already proven myself as an articulate, polished guest.

At this point, I had successfully hit my goal of making 250 videos in the space of a year and was no longer afraid of appearing on camera. It was time to turn my attention to developing another skill, the skill of giving a great interview.

As I'd previously done with my videos, I gave myself a simple, measurable goal, to reach out to five podcasters per day, five days a week.

I often sent my outreach emails at night right before I went to bed. Why? In many ways, it's the worst time of day to reach out because if anyone responded, I wouldn't be able to follow up until the next morning. The emails went out at night because they were so far outside my comfort zone that I kept pushing them off. But because I'd made a commitment to myself, I had to send them before heading to sleep.

As with the videos, I kept reminding myself that small, deliberate actions taken regularly pay off. And when I started out writing these messages, I didn't exactly know what I was doing. As evidence of my ineptitude, here is how Doc Green, host of the *Earn and Invest* podcast, introduced me on his show:

"I have to admit, I was a little bit skeptical of Dave Mason. He wrote me over Facebook and said, 'Hey, I've got this book. I want to be on your podcast to talk about it. It's called *The Cash Machine*. I was like 'yeah, whatever, send me the book, I'll take a look, and then I'll consider.' A week later, the book comes in the mail. It's a Saturday, I have nothing to do. I sit down for a few minutes to read while I'm in between things. Four hours later I look up and I'm done."

As Doc's intro implies, my first outreach emails were sorely lacking, but as with my videos, they gradually got better. And podcasters know podcasters, so as I did interviews, I'd ask the hosts for introductions to other podcasters. My interview with Doc Green, for instance, helped me get on Joe Saul-Sehy's *Stacking Benjamins* show, which Kiplinger had rated as the top finance podcast. And later, when I ran my own financial summit, both these hosts became my guests.

Gigantic failures sting. If all your hopes come down to one final Hail Mary pass, to one winner takes all bet, to one pitch that will either make or break your business, then you risk disaster.

Far better to engineer many small failures than risk a big one. The vast majority of my podcaster outreach emails were failures. Less than half of those I contacted even responded, and less than half of those who wrote back expressed interest. Each one of those emails that didn't yield an interview was a failure, but it was a small failure, one that barely stung at all, and that was ultimately overshadowed by successes.

Instead of sending out five pitches a day, I could have spent months preparing the perfect pitch to one of the world's top podcasters and based my entire strategy on landing that one show. In that scenario, I wouldn't have received daily feedback on my pitch emails, I wouldn't have practiced my interview skills day after day, I wouldn't have honed my process or built my network. My odds of failing in that one epic pitch would have been tremendous and the impact debilitating.

If you want to get started engineering these small failures, the following strategies can help:

1. **Define your commitment.** What is it you're willing to do? Publish a video each day? Network with 10 people a day? Your commitment needs to be measurable such that you'll know each day if you accomplished it or not.

2. **Avoid perfectionism.** Especially in your early efforts, just getting it done can be an accomplishment. Don't set the bar so high that it blocks you from taking daily action.

3. **Establish consistent routines.** Do you take action first thing in the morning? Last thing at night? Consistency helps your actions stick and develop into a habit.

4. **Pair the new habit with an existing one.** If you love your morning smoothie, you can drink it while sending your outreach emails. Or you can use that same smoothie as a reward for recording your daily video. Either way, the engrained habit can help you embed the new one.

5. **Keep upping your game.** When I first started making daily videos, just recording them was a victory. Later victories came from improving my sound, lighting, and my process for creating content. Remember, this is a process for growth and you want your results to continually improve.

In Part 1, we discussed the need to embrace failure. Fear of failure makes us play it safe, and very little learning and growth occurs in our safety zone. The more we delight in our failures, the more we can stretch ourselves and get into that arena where learning and growth prosper.

In Part 2, we saw that we can engineer failure to derive maximum benefit. Once you've entered the Death Zone on Mount Everest, the stakes of failing are far too high. We get the most benefit from our failures when they occur rapidly and with little risk.

Of course, the point of engineering failure is to learn from it. Failure alone doesn't guarantee improvement. Even worse, we can walk away having learning the wrong lessons. That's why in Part 3 we're going to explore how to most effectively learn from our failures.

 Assess your own ability to Hurry Up and Fail and identify your own failure blindspots by taking our Failure Scorecard at **DaveMasonAuthor.com/failure-scorecard**

PART 3
Learning from Failure

CHAPTER 7

Seek Feedback

*"If at first you don't succeed, destroy
all evidence that you tried."*

— STEVEN WRIGHT

Mark Watney desperately needs heat. Actually, as an American astronaut left for dead on Mars, what he desperately needs is a radio capable of communicating with Earth. And he knows where to find one. In 1996, NASA had launched the Carl Sagan Memorial Station, better known as Pathfinder, to explore the surface of Mars. NASA had long since lost contact with the antiquated Martian probe, but if Watney can find the probe and get it working again, he could send a distress signal to Earth and let NASA know he's still alive. He has enough solar cells to power his Mars Rover for the drive to Pathfinder. It wouldn't be fast. Most of the day would be spent recharging the batteries just to fuel a couple of hours of driving. But he could do it. His problem is keeping warm in the frigid Martian atmosphere, which would require more than half the Rover's battery power and undermine his ability to make the drive in time. He has a solution, but the risks are terrifying.

For anyone not familiar, this scenario is taken from the seventh chapter of Andy Weir's brilliant book, *The Martian*, later made into a movie starring Matt Damon. Before reading *The Martian*, I'd thought of science fiction as fictional science. *Star Wars* and *Star Trek* adhere to scientific laws only when convenient. As one comic put it, "Science fiction that follows the law of relativity is relatively boring." But *The Martian* is different. I think of it as *MacGyver* in space, and Andy's adherence to the constraints of science and technology make the book both thrilling and educational.

Hurry Up and Fail

Back to Watney's need for heat. His solution? Using the RTG. What's an RTG? I'll let Watney explain in his own words:

'The RTG (radioisotope thermoelectric generator) is a big box of plutonium. But not the kind used in nuclear bombs. No, no. This plutonium is way more dangerous!

Plutonium-238 is an incredibly unstable isotope. It's so radioactive that it will get red hot all by itself. As you can imagine, a material that can literally fry an egg with radiation is kind of dangerous.

…As long ago as the 1960s, NASA began using RTGs to power unmanned probes… But they never used RTGs on manned missions until the Ares Program.

Why not? It should be pretty obvious why not! They didn't want to put astronauts next to a glowing hot ball of radioactive death!'

In *The Martian*, the RTG is only intended to power activities on Mars until the astronauts arrive. As soon as they land, one of the first things they do is bury the RTG four kilometers away from their base, where it could cause them no harm.

One thing Andy Weir does exceptionally well in *The Martian* is to connect readers to Mark Watney's emotional rollercoaster. Being stranded for years on an unfriendly planet while living in quarters only intended to support human life for 30 days puts him in constant risk of death. And he doesn't just need to survive, he has to constantly solve problems, including how to communicate with Earth, feed himself, and get off the planet.

The RTG can provide Watney with more than enough heat to keep warm during his trip, but Watney is freaked out by the prospect of using it. He'd almost died once while making water from rocket fuel, and he's convinced using the RTG will "be far more dangerous."

The book is a nail-biter. It's funny, thrilling, and clever. But I have to admit, if there was one segment where I didn't feel emotional resonance with Mark Watney, it was this segment with the RTG. Somehow, I couldn't feel his fear with the "glowing hot ball of radioactive death" that would make NASA engineers "hide under their desks and cuddle with their slide rules for comfort." It was only during an email correspondence with Andy Weir during the writing of this book that I finally understood why this one segment failed to resonate, and I came away with even greater respect for Andy's integrity as a writer.

Few movie companies have enjoyed as much success right out of the gates as did Pixar, the digital animation studio purchased by Steve Jobs in 1986, soon after Apple gave him the boot. Their initial release, *Toy Story*, was the first ever feature film created exclusively with digital animation and became the second highest grossing film of 1995. Pixar followed that with hit movies *A Bug's Life*, *Toy Story 2*, and *Monster's Inc.* Disney had an exclusive contract to distribute Pixar films, and enjoyed huge profits from Pixar's early success. When the contract between Disney and Pixar drew near its close, there was no question Disney wanted to renew their arrangement with the groundbreaking animation company.

But there was still a question of timing. If Disney negotiated the new contract on the heels of a hit film, they'd pay a lot more than if the negotiation followed a flop. No movie studio produces only hits without its periodic failures. Surely Pixar, which had four hits in a row, would be due a failure soon, right?

That's what the board at Disney wanted to know. If the next movie was going to be a hit, they were better off signing a deal before its release. But if it were a dud, they'd save millions by waiting until after its release. Fortunately, they had the perfect way to find out. Michael Eisner, the iconic Disney Chairman and CEO, was going to visit Pixar and would check their latest film's progress.

Afterwards, Eisner emailed the Disney board reporting the following:

Yesterday we saw for the second time the new Pixar movie 'Finding Nemo' that comes out next May. This will be a reality check for those guys. It's okay, but nowhere near as good as their previous films. Of course, they think it is great.

The board, trusting in Eisner's ability to assess the caliber of an animated feature, took his advice to wait. Huge mistake. *Finding Nemo* won the Oscar for Best Animated Feature and became the highest grossing animated film of all time.

How had Eisner gotten it so wrong?

In the Steve Jobs biography by Walter Isaacson, this story is used to illustrate how Eisner had grown out of touch with audiences. Certainly, if he could so thoroughly miscalculate the success of the highest grossing animated movie of all time, then he had no business being the head of Disney, a company built on its domination of the animated movie market.

But not so fast. Is it possible Eisner's judgment wasn't so poor? Remember, Eisner didn't see the version of *Finding Nemo* that rocked the box office. He saw a *draft*. And Eisner wasn't known for his intimacy with the Pixar team. As Jobs recounts:

During the twenty-year relationship, he visited Pixar for a total of about two and a half hours, only to give congratulatory speeches. He was never curious. I was amazed. Curiosity is very important.

Had he been curious, he would have learned that Pixar operated differently from the animation department at Disney. "Early on, *all* our movies suck," Pixar cofounder Ed Catmull writes in his book *Creativity, Inc*. "We are true believers in the power of bracing, candid feedback, and the iterative process—reworking, reworking, and reworking again, until a flawed story finds its through-line or a hollow character finds its soul."

Two of Pixar's strongest tools for this feedback are the BrainTrust and Dailies. The BrainTrust brings together Pixar's heavy hitters to review the progress of a movie in development every few months. As Pixar director and BrainTrust member Andrew Stanton likes to say, "If Pixar is a hospital and the movies are the patients, then the Braintrust is made up of trusted doctors." Bob Peterson, another member of the Braintrust, compares it to "The grand eye of Sauron." But Catmull is quick to point out that unlike Sauron, "The Braintrust is benevolent. It wants to help. And it has no selfish agenda."

Catmull calls early versions of their stories *ugly babies*. "They are not beautiful, miniature versions of the adults they will grow up to be. They are truly ugly: awkward and unformed, vulnerable and incomplete. They need nurturing—in the form of time and patience—in order to grow." Catmull says the Braintrust is crucial to this process. "The BrainTrust is where we figure out why they suck, and it's also where they start to not suck."

The BrainTrust is a blunt instrument. Within its sphere, entire storylines drop away. But at Pixar, they don't just have feedback sessions every few months when the BrainTrust convenes. Each day, teams at Pixar get together to critique everything developed the day before. "The Dailies keep everyone in top form," Director Mark Andrews says. "It's an intimidating room to be in because the goal is to create the best animation possible. We go through every single frame with a fine-toothed comb, over and over and over again."

For example, take the following sequence from the movie *Brave*, in which one of the main characters transforms into a bear. In the Dailies, Andrews was bothered by a ten frame sequence of the bear walking. "She looks like she's stepping more catlike than heavy-bear-like," he said. "I like the overall speed, but I'm not feeling the weight. She's walking like a ninja."

For context, ten frames in a movie is less than half a second long. Is your experience of a movie going to change all that much based on how a bear is walking during that fraction of a second? Most studios probably wouldn't bother analyzing it, let alone fixing it. But at Pixar, where getting each detail right is an obsession, the animators went back to adjust the bear's gait.

Which brings us back to *Finding Nemo*, the movie Eisner thought would be Pixar's first disaster. The Pixar team had just gone through an excruciating process with *Toy Story 2*, a movie originally slated as a low budget direct-to-video film that Pixar completely remade for theatrical release. Their now famous feedback mechanisms, the BrainTrust and Dailies, had yet to be perfected. Indeed, at the time, rather than seeking more feedback, they desired a process with less. The eleventh hour changes in *Toy Story 2* were so stressful, they wanted to get the story right the first time and dispense with the need for major edits later on.

As Catmull recounts, "Looking back, I realize we weren't just trying to be more efficient. We were hoping to avoid the messy (and at times uncomfortable) part of the creative process." The creative process can be messy. Getting honest feedback can be uncomfortable. But *Nemo* just wasn't coming together. A series of flashbacks, which had sounded great during the pitch stage, didn't have the desired effect in early versions of the movie, coming across, as one BrainTrust member called them, as "cryptic and impressionistic." The main character, Marlin, initially felt unsympathetic and unlikeable, but when flashbacks were replaced by a more linear script, one that showed from the beginning why Marlin was so terrified of losing his son to the dangers of the ocean, the story flowed better and Marlin became more appealing.

As much as the Pixar team wanted to get *Finding Nemo* right the first time, they realized such expectations weren't realistic if they wanted to produce their best work. If creating great films was the goal, they needed to be open to feedback and be willing to make the changes when necessary, both on the large scale (through the BrainTrust) and the small scale (through Dailies).

Andy Weir, author of *The Martian*, describes himself as a lifelong space nerd whose hobbies include relativistic physics, orbital mechanics, and the history of manned spaceflight. With a biography like that, you might expect Andy's career path to include astronaut or mechanical engineer at NASA. But, perhaps due to his fear of flying, he never worked in the space sector, instead becoming a programmer for AOL, Palm, and others. Still, he never stopped devoting his free time to his love of space.

Like all authors, I'm sure Andy dreamt of his novel taking off and becoming a massive hit. But in the initial stages, authors can be extremely secretive about their books. I worked on my first book for years before anyone other than my wife even knew I was trying my hand as a writer. Most authors reveal their work carefully, perhaps only showing early drafts to a trusted loved one for feedback, as I did with my wife, Chana. Slowly, the inner circle expands. The next reader might be an editor. Agents and publishers have to wait for another draft or two before getting a glimpse. Reviewers come in late in the game, when the book is in near publishable form. Finally, after much fanfare and a well-anticipated launch, the public finally gets their hands on it.

But Andy didn't write this way. When he completed each chapter, he posted it for free on his personal website. As he told me, "I had about 3,000 regular readers at the time, most of them hardcore nerds. When I got something wrong on science, I'd get a bunch of emails telling me about it."

Personally, I cringe at the idea of putting any of my early stage writing out for public consumption. But Andy was writing a book that delved into extremely complex science. He wasn't just dealing with run-of-the-mill astrophysics. He delved into obscure questions like how botany functions on Mars. For one person to understand every complexity is no simple feat. And if Andy erred in obscure areas of science, ordinary editors would never catch them. But a community of 3000 hardcore nerds is an entirely different story.

I asked Andy for examples where audience feedback forced a change to his story. Lo and behold, he came back with our old friend, the RTG. "A nuclear engineer on a US Navy submarine told me about radiation. The RTG, which generates heat, does so via radiation. I had a lot of stuff in there about the dangers of what would happen if the RTG broke open. Turns out that was all wrong. The Navy guy told me RTGs are full of small radioactive beads surrounded by lead. So even if the RTG did break open, Mark would be safe."

When I read this email, I finally understood why the RTG segment didn't unnerve me the way Mark's other near-death challenges did. In the original draft, no doubt the presence of the RTG makes Mark feel he's always a hairsbreadth away from death. But because Andy had this nuclear engineer among his early readers, he learned his assumptions were wrong. Andy had a choice to make. He could keep the scene in its original nail-biting form. After all, it's hardly necessary to explain every safety measure when writing a novel. Or he could undermine the drama in the name of accuracy.

I faced a similar situation with my personal finance novel, *The Cash Machine*, except, unlike Andy, I didn't learn about my mistake until after publication. The error involved a minor nuance in an obscure law dealing with tax breaks for Americans who live and work abroad. The misquoted segment likely would have impacted exactly 0% of my readers. But it was wrong, and that irked me. I wound up putting out a new edition of the book with the corrected text to get it right.

Had Andy decided the plutonium pellets in his RTG weren't coated with protective lead, virtually no one would have noticed. Or he could've neglected to explain how the lead coating protects the radioactive pellets so readers would still experience a heightened sense of tension, even if the fictional Watney isn't in as much danger as we think. But my gut tells me being even slightly off on the science bothered Andy the same way being slightly off on the tax code irked me. So he changed the passage, opting for accuracy over emotion.

Stop a moment and think about this RTG mistake. If it hadn't been corrected in draft form, how likely is it this error would have been identified and corrected at all? Certainly no mortal editor would have caught it. Perhaps if Andy had hired a scientific fact checker to go over each and every detail, it could have been unearthed, but there's so much science in the novel and the construction of the RTG is so obscure, even then it likely would have passed by unnoticed.

Most likely, Andy would have published *The Martian* with the RTG mistake intact. Perhaps then, someone like the nuclear submarine engineer would have pointed out the mistake, but perhaps not. I periodically uncover mistakes in books, but I don't write to authors to tell them because by the time I've caught the error, they've already moved on to their next project. Andy didn't just release *The Martian* early to 3000 nerds, he did so in a way that encouraged dialog and feedback. This is extremely rare. Fixing an error when it's at the blog post phase is easy. Fixing a published bestseller is difficult. The ability to tap into such a knowledgeable community early on became a huge asset for Andy Weir to make his book so accurate and authentic.

Feedback can truly be a gift. It's easy to fall in love with the dream of being the genius who works behind locked doors, who emerges and awes the world with the perfect creation. But that's rarely a recipe for creating greatness. When we open ourselves up to feedback, we get many minds working instead of one, and our early failures can become our greatest successes.

In Pixar's case, they built two powerful feedback mechanisms into their creative process. The BrainTrust brought together the heavy hitters in the company every few months to review each project. This is where entire story lines would be slashed and otherwise promising films sent back to the drawing board. But they didn't just have a macro feedback loop that examined their projects once every few months. They also had the Dailies, a micro feedback loop that examined the prior day's work and made minor changes along the way.

Pixar could build these feedback loops because they're a large organization filled with obsessive creatives. But as we saw from Andy Weir, even an individual working alone can find effective ways to get feedback, even in the early stages of a project.

If you're looking to build a robust feedback process, the following tips can help:

1. **Everyone is an expert on what they like and dislike, but don't expect everyone to articulate why.** I discovered this with the early drafts of my first novel. Readers would tell me when they thought a scene wasn't working and offer advice for improvement. These readers were always right about which scenes just didn't work, but most of the time their suggestions for how to improve it only made the issue worse. I needed a seasoned editor to tell me how to make the improvements.

2. **Ask specific questions.** The feedback providers may give more valuable insights if they know exactly what questions you want answered.

3. **Create a safe space.** If you get defensive with each criticism, you may stop getting honest feedback. Allowing feedback to be given anonymously can also help.

4. **Act on the feedback and follow up.** If those giving feedback see that you're implementing their advice and updating them on the process, they're more likely to see their efforts as valuable and want to continue helping.

Just like we saw in Part 2 that failures provide the most opportunity for learning when they happen quickly and with little downside, so too with feedback it can be most impactful when received early on and in small doses.

If you're currently working on a project, ask yourself how you can create shorter, more effective feedback loops. Ideally, you want to be receiving feedback on your work as early as possible. Unfortunately, as we'll see in the next chapter, most feedback loops are not built this way and may only kick in after catastrophic disaster.

CHAPTER 8

Investigate Failure

*"The only real mistake is the one
from which we learn nothing."*

- HENRY FORD

Living in Jerusalem, in a highly international community, there's nothing unusual about having a friend traveling out of the country. I'm used to seeing Facebook posts with pictures of one of my neighbors on a beach in Thailand or in some small African village, or back in the US visiting parents. The destinations are periodically a big deal, but except for the early COVID days, we were all boarding airplanes so often that the flights themselves were not. Perhaps that's why it stuck in my mind when my friend Jonathan posted a picture of himself standing in front of the plane he was about to board on March 10, 2019, an Ethiopian Air flight from Addis Ababa, Ethiopia to Nairobi, Kenya on his way to the United Nations Environment Assembly. I couldn't help wondering what compelled him to post a picture of himself in front of the airplane and share his flight details?

I only wondered at this for a second before scrolling on. After all, unusual posts are not that unusual. I didn't think of it again until a few hours later when I heard that Ethiopian Air flight ET302 from Addis Ababa to Nairobi had crashed.

In early 1994, our newly formed Colorado College Chess Club played a match against a local Colorado Springs club. Our coach arranged the evening despite knowing we were seriously outmatched, and in doing so, employed many of the Hurry Up and Fail principles we've already discussed. He wanted us to start before we were ready and pit ourselves against far superior opponents so we could see how much more we had to learn.

Predictably, we got creamed. Every single one of my teammates lost. In my match, I was playing black and was doing OK. My opponent used an opening I'd never seen before, but I countered it as best as I could, and after 45 minutes, the pieces were still even. Our club coach said he wanted to talk to me privately. My opponent immediately objected.

Our coach was a chess master. When recruiting for the club, he arranged tables around himself in a rectangle configuration, set up 12 chess boards, and invited all challengers. Over the next hour, he easily defeated over 50 students, playing a dozen games at a time. There was no doubt he could destroy my current opponent. But this wasn't a football game where the coach could call a time out and have a one-on-one with the quarterback. Chess isn't a team sport, and it seemed wrong for him to jump in and coach me on strategy.

My coach assured my opponent and me that this was perfectly normal, and he wouldn't give me any moves. What he said instead was simple, yet somehow I missed it. He said I should offer my opponent a draw. If he accepted, we'd still leave the evening winless, but at least avoid losing *every* game. Unfortunately, I misunderstood, thinking he wanted me to play *for* a draw, something I'd no idea how to do.

The interchange left me flustered and confused. My defense quickly fell apart, and I lost within minutes.

But my big revelation for the night was still to come. During our game, my opponent and I recorded our moves. After defeating me and shaking my hand, my opponent set up the board anew. He then used our recordings to review the game step by step. He explained the opening he used and why he liked it. He even said my impromptu defense used his preferred counter against that attack. Of course, my off-the-cuff moves didn't follow his preferred defense for long. He asked me what I was trying to achieve with my tactics and showed me alternatives that might have worked better.

Then we got to the disastrous turning point where I abandoned my strategy and tried to play for a draw. He showed me the end game tactics that might have worked better, though he also explained why, despite having the same pieces, his position was already better and would have led to victory even if my defense hadn't collapsed.

This process is known in chess circles as a post-mortem. Post-mortem is Latin for "after death." Medically, it's another term for an autopsy, an examination of a corpse to determine the time and cause of death. In chess, the post-mortem is a primary teaching tool. My opponent during the match became my teacher after it. We reexamined my moves, identifying where I went wrong and how I could do better.

During that first post-mortem, I mostly listened and asked questions, lacking the knowledge to help my opponent improve his own game. But from that point on, the post-mortem became a regular tool in my toolbox, both for chess and beyond.

In the early 1950s, the world was just entering the age of jet-powered commercial flight. Jet planes flew faster, higher, and quieter than their propeller-powered predecessors. But the new technology brought new challenges. Crashes were not uncommon, and the wreckage left few clues as to what went wrong.

In 1953, following multiple mysterious crashes of the *de Havilland Comet* airliners, Australian David Warren decided to do something about it. He realized our ability to make planes safer was severely inhibited by our failure to understand why they crashed. Post-mortem investigations suffered from a lack of data. His idea was simple, even if the technology behind it was not. He wanted a way of recording what happened in a plane before a crash that could be recovered post-crash so an investigative team could accurately assess its cause.

His solution was to create a Flight Data Recorder (FDR) so solid it could survive a plane crash. Early FDRs contained up to four hours of audio recordings as well as data including the plane's heading, altitude, airspeed, vertical accelerations, and the time. Warren initially received pushback as detractors claimed recording cockpit conversations would violate a pilot's right to privacy. But as jetliners continued to fall out of the sky, privacy issues became secondary. Before long, Warren's FDRs were mandated on virtually all commercial flights. Though colored a bright orange to make them easy to spot amongst the wreckage, the FDRs are colloquially known as "black boxes," and have been instrumental in advancing airline safety.

I started this chapter with a story about my friend, Jonathan, the one traveling Ethiopian Air. He arrived safely in Nairobi blissfully unaware friends and family around the world were in a panic and thought they'd lost him. He learned upon landing that a different Ethiopian flight from Addis Ababa to Nairobi, the one that had taken off directly before his, hadn't made it. All 157 passengers and crew died, including over a dozen who were also traveling to the United Nations Environment Assembly meeting.

Hurry Up and Fail

The plane was brand new, the pilot well-trained and experienced, the weather was clear. So what had gone wrong?

The history of air travel contains more than its share of freak accidents. But many suspected this crash was more than an anomaly. Why? Because the circumstances of the Ethiopian disaster were eerily similar to a crash less than a year earlier on Lion Air Flight JT610 from Jakarta to Pangkal Pinang. Both flights crashed within minutes of taking off. And both flights were on identical equipment, the newly released Boeing 737 Max.

Ethiopian Airlines Flight ET302 wasn't one of those crash landings where the pilot glides the plane down and lands it as softly as possible. This plane dove at a 40-degree angle, hitting the ground at over 500 miles per hour, hard enough to leave a crater 32 feet deep, and so utterly destroying the aircraft that few pieces of the wreckage remained large enough to tell they once belonged to a plane.

From 2010 to 2019, approximately 57% percent of all airline crashes were attributed to pilot error, 21% to mechanical problems, and 10% to adverse weather conditions. In actuality, few of these crashes involved just one factor. For instance, a pilot may make a poor choice when flying into strong winds, but do we conclude the crash was due to poor weather or to pilot error? As safety expert Sidney Dekker says, human error is not an explanation. Human error demands explanation.

No investigation has rocked the aviation industry in recent memory more than that of the Boeing 737 Max aircraft. When the black box data from flights ET302 and JT610 were analyzed, they didn't reveal anything as innocuous as a pilot error or poor weather. They revealed a defect in the *entire industry*.

If you read the crash reports, you'll discover two flaws that in combination brought down both flights. The first was a faulty sensor, which relayed incorrect data to the computer. The second was an onboard computer system called the Maneuvering Characteristics Augmentation System (MCAS) which tried to stabilize the airplanes. But since the MCAS was relying on faulty data, it doomed the planes instead. This might be humanity's second biggest fear with artificial intelligence. When computers have so much power over our lives, one faulty instruction or incorrect data point can lead to disaster. (For humanity's number one fear with AI, see *Terminator, The*)

When the pilots discovered their planes were trying to kill them, couldn't they have turned off the MCAS? In theory, yes. However, both crashes occurred soon after takeoff. There wasn't much time to react. More importantly, the

Ethiopian pilots weren't well trained on how to deal with the MCAS, and the Lion Air pilots didn't know it was there at all. Before you conclude this resulted from poor training from third world airlines, it wasn't. Boeing intentionally hid its very existence.

It seems counterintuitive that Boeing wouldn't want pilots trained on how to recover from an MCAS error. But like airline crashes, horrible business decisions are often not the result of one factor alone. Boeing felt pressure from at least two different parties, a competitor and a client.

Airbus and Boeing are the world's two largest airplane manufacturers by a wide margin. They're in constant competition for contracts from major airlines, and when either gains a technological advantage, the other feels tremendous pressure to match it.

On December 1, 2010, Airbus released the A320neo. As a passenger, when I think about airplane improvements, I care most about the comfort of seats, legroom, and entertainment options. But to airlines, there's a far bigger concern: fuel efficiency. For perspective, according to the Southwest Airlines 2012 annual report, fuel costs reached 6.156 billion dollars, making up 37.3% of their annual operating expenses.

The A320neo shocked the airline industry by offering 15% to 20% better fuel efficiency on a per-seat basis than the prior A320 model. It also promised to be at least 6% more efficient than Boeing's airplane in the same class, the 737. Let's apply these savings to Southwest, who posted profits of $417 million in 2012. If Southwest cut just 6% of its 6.156 billion dollar fuel bill, they would have saved over $369 million, increasing their $417 million profit to $786 million, a spike in profitability of over 88%. This wasn't a small development; it was a game changer. Boeing could do nothing but watch as the Airbus A320neo became the fastest selling aircraft in history, dealing more in a single week at the 2011 Paris Air Show than Boeing had sold 737s in all of 2010.

Boeing needed a new plane to compete with the A320neo, and they needed it fast. Designing a whole new airliner no doubt would have given the company its best chance at technologically outperforming the A320neo. But that would take years and cost billions. With their market share slipping fast, they couldn't afford delays. Instead, they decided to quickly revamp the 46-year-old 737.

Unfortunately for Boeing, there was a key distinction between the Airbus A320 and their own 737 that made the A320 easier to revamp. The A320 rides higher when it's on the ground, which left room to fit a larger, more fuel-efficient breed of engine under the wing. Boeing couldn't easily make the same improvement because of the lack of space under the 737's wings.

Hurry Up and Fail

Time was of the essence. To compete in the marketplace, Boeing needed to produce new engines that could fit on their old, low-riding plane. They came up with a solution, albeit an imperfect one. To mount the larger engines on the wings and still have enough clearance below the engines, they made the top of the engines stick up over the top of the wings. This caused the airplanes to have too much lift when in a steep climb. Too much lift can increase what's called the Angle of Attack, the angle at which the plane diverges from the flow of the surrounding air. If the Angle of Attack exceeds 18 to 20 degrees, a plane is in serious danger of stalling.

There were quite a few potential solutions to this problem, but another restraint limited Boeing's options.

Let's go back to Southwest for a moment. If you've ever flown Southwest, you know they operate far differently than the old-school airlines like United, American, and Delta. Southwest changed the boarding process and seat assignments, and they eliminated first class and meal service. Why? Because Southwest is an efficiency machine.

In 2019, Southwest recorded its 47th straight year of profitability, something unheard of in the traditionally anemic airline industry. I keep waiting for more airlines to copy Southwest's playbook, because they're clearly doing something right; but strangely, they've remained an outlier. Their obsession with efficiency goes way beyond innovative boarding and seating plans. One of their biggest distinctions is that they only fly one model of plane: the Boeing 737.

How does keeping their entire fleet flying 737s help? It means all key components are interchangeable. If one plane has mechanical issues, simply bring in another. You don't have to worry about some flight crews being trained on one piece of equipment and others on different planes. All crews are interchangeable. The mechanics only have to work on one model of plane. You only need to keep spare parts for the 737, which cuts down on inventory and increases the odds of having what you need on hand.

As thrilled as Southwest must have been to learn Boeing was working on an upgrade with better fuel efficiency, they also had one concern. They made it clear to Boeing that they would only buy the 737 Max if it flew exactly like their other 737s. In fact, they negotiated a clause in their purchase contract for the new planes stating Boeing would owe them a rebate of one million dollars per plane if Southwest was required to train their pilots to fly them.

It wasn't only to satisfy Southwest that Boeing felt pressure to keep the flying experience exactly the same as on the older 737s. Pilots don't simply shift from flying a 737 one day to a 747 the next. The planes are different, the

Investigate Failure

cockpits are different, the controls are different. Switching from one plane to another poses the risk of pilots getting confused when under stress, and when pilots get confused, people can die. Pilots need to be rated by the FAA for each type of plane they fly, and they're normally only rated for one type at a time. If Boeing could make the new 737 Max fly exactly like the old 737, they could claim it should be included under the existing FAA 737 rating. Otherwise, the FAA might assign the 737 Max a new rating class, which would limit who could fly them, raise training costs, and undermine orders. In other words, Boeing needed a solution for the stalling problem that would ideally be undetectable to pilots and not require additional training.

Their solution was a secret software override that would kick in when the 737 Max detected too much lift. The MCAS would take control, forcing the nose downwards until the Angle of Attack returned to safe levels. Pilots were neither trained to handle the new software nor even informed it existed.

But what would happen if the sensors measuring the Angle of Attack returned incorrect data? What if the software believed the plane had too much lift, when in actuality, the plane was perfectly safe? In such a scenario, the software would keep pushing the nose of the plane down until the plane was in a steep dive toward the ground below, and its untrained pilot would have no clue how to react.

Was Boeing blissfully unaware of this potential flaw in the 737 Max until the planes starting falling out of the sky? Unfortunately, no. Boeing admits it knew about the problem a year before the Lion Air crash, but still took no action.

A week after the first crash, the pilots finally heard the 737 Max had a "flight control system" that could cause pilots to have "difficulty controlling the airplane" and result in "possible impact with terrain."

Nevertheless, Boeing was still reluctant to release information about the MCAS or take any steps to correct the problem. Simultaneously, they informed pilots they were the backups if the MCAS system failed. But how could they be the backups for a system they knew nothing about?

Pilots weren't reassured by either of these statements. As they told Boeing, "We flat out deserve to know what is on our airplanes."

The FAA didn't ground the 737 Max planes, but did issue a directive to pilots to turn off the MCAS system if they ever witnessed it trying to send the plane into a steep dive. The Ethiopian Air pilots had received the directive, but no one informed them they'd only have ten seconds to shut the faulty system down. By the time they managed to get it offline, it was too late to recover.

Freak accidents occur in air travel. Black box analysis helps engineers identify errors, and periodic tweaks are made to prevent a recurrence. But when

Ethiopian Airlines Flight ET302 went down, the Lion Air crash could no longer be written off as a freak accident. This was now a pattern, and it was a pattern involving Boeing's newest and best-selling aircraft.

All 387 functioning 737 Max aircraft, which served 8,600 flights per week for 59 airlines, were grounded by March 18, 2019. The groundings continued for 20 months, the longest ever grounding of a US airliner. Boeing was forced to pay an estimated $20 billion in compensation to airlines and victims' families, lost business, and legal fees, in addition to losing more than $60 billion from 1,200 canceled orders.

The results of the 737 Max black box investigations were damning, not just to Boeing, but to the airline industry as a whole. The FAA admitted it never fully analyzed the MCAS system prior to certifying the 737 Max as fit for flight. In fact, much of the responsibility for certifying the safety of the planes has been shifted in recent years from the FAA to the plane manufacturers themselves. In other words, the regulatory system meant to keep the airline industry honest and passengers safe has been largely outsourced to the very people who have a financial incentive to manipulate the system. The black box analysis didn't just reveal a technical problem on the 737 Max, it showcased a weakness in our entire regulatory and safety system.

Post-mortem investigations are excellent ways to learn from failures. In this chapter, we looked at post-mortem investigations through two very different lenses, one of them a low-stakes failure, the other a high-stakes disaster.

After losing my chess match, the post-mortem gave me insights into my opponent's mind, allowing me to understand his strategies and see the flaws in my own. My chess game advanced more in that one post-mortem than it would in a year of casually playing.

The Boeing 737 Max investigation likewise showed the immense power of post-mortems as a tool for learning from failure. However, in this case, there was no Hurrying Up and Failing. Boeing didn't welcome feedback on their new system, nor did they actively look to expose its flaws so they could correct them. Rather, they attempted to hide known flaws, which meant that when failure did come, it came in catastrophic form.

The next time you're involved in a failure, don't just move on and try again. Consider conducting a post-mortem and really examining where things went wrong. The following questions can help you clarify the causes of failure and make better adjustments in the future:

Investigate Failure

1. **When did you first detect your effort was likely to fail?** Did you immediately take action to get back on the right track or did you avoid facing the failure?

2. **What was the root cause of your failure?**

3. **Who was involved in the failure?** Was there someone working on the project who shouldn't have been? Was there someone who should have been involved who wasn't?

4. **What was the impact of the failure?**

5. **Were any steps taken to mitigate the consequences of the failure?** Were there additional steps that could have been taken but weren't?

6. **What lessons did you learn from the failure?**

7. **With all this information in hand, how will you proceed differently next time?**

The above is just a partial list of questions you can ask as you go through a post-mortem investigation, but I hope they already show how powerful this tool can be in learning from failure.

Of course, the big limitations with post-mortems is that they first require you to fail. If you Hurry Up and Fail, intentionally creating frequent, low-stakes failures, that's not such a problem. Still, it's not always easy to engineer low-stakes failures.

Wouldn't it be great if we could get the benefits of the post-mortem investigation without having to first go through the actual failure? What if we could see impending disaster and avoid it in advance? Just as hindsight is not 20/20, foresight isn't either. But there is a tool that brings us closer.

CHAPTER 9

Forsee Failure

"Every adversity, every failure, every heartache carries with it the seed of an equal or greater benefit."

- NAPOLEON HILL

In July 1998, I stood outside Interpol headquarters in Lyon, France, confident in how to blow up the building. Interpol had been bombed once before, in 1986. The explosion caused significant damage but failed to bring down the old headquarters in Paris. The new headquarters in Lyon was far more secure. Or so the organization claimed. But I'd found a vulnerability. Not that I had much power to take action. Fortunately, I wasn't standing outside Interpol alone, and my companion had all the influence I lacked.

I was nervous to share my strategy as I questioned how responsive my companion would be. So I backed into it with: "Hey Ron, if you wanted to blow up Interpol, could you do it?"

"Easily," he responded.

"How?"

Ron dove into an explanation of his tactics. His plan lacked subtlety, to say the least, which told me he was unaware of the security vulnerability I'd found. Most importantly, his voice remained light and conversational. That was a good sign. I'd been afraid he'd chew my head off for broaching the subject, but once I heard how he'd proceed with his own strategy, I knew he'd be willing to listen to mine.

Affable as Ron normally came across, he wasn't one to be trifled with. I'd learned that the hard way when I'd first applied to work with him. My roommate had told me to include a conversation piece on my resume, so I added a blurb about backpacking around the world and included a list of the countries visited.

"I see you've been to Cuba," Ron said after looking over the resume. "Do you know the legal penalty for a US citizen traveling to Cuba?"

This conversation starter was proving a little too effective, and I didn't like the direction this was going. I knew I'd broken US law when I'd entered Cuba in the winter of 1996, but hadn't considered it a big deal. I'd never looked into the exact penalty if caught. But Ron knew. And he started telling me the consequences I could have faced. In detail.

Though he was a law professor, I was surprised by his legal knowledge in this area. I doubted anyone else at NYU Law would have had a clue about the issue. "You seem to know an awful lot about the penalties for going to Cuba," I said.

"Well, that was my branch of government," Ron replied.

This interview just kept going downhill. "Let me get this straight," I said. "You used to work for the branch of the government in charge of arresting me when I went to Cuba?"

"No, Dave. I used to *run* the branch of the government in charge of arresting you when you went to Cuba."

Google didn't yet exist, but it didn't take me long to research the true identity of this mild-mannered law professor. Ronald K. Noble, former Undersecretary of the Treasury for Defense, in charge of the Secret Service, the Customs Service, and the Division of Alcohol, Tobacco, and Firearms (all of which are now under the Department of Homeland Security).

My initial fears that my visit to Cuba would cost me the job proved unfounded. Ron wanted to hire an assistant to help him with a mission that summer at Interpol, and the last thing he wanted was someone he'd have to babysit. He later told me my backpacking experience was key to landing the job. He figured I'd have no problem looking after myself in a foreign country.

And that's how we came to be standing outside Interpol a few months later, discussing how to blow it up. Once Ron finished telling me how he'd take down the building, I launched into my own strategy, complete with a description of the security vulnerability I'd found.

"No, that can't be," he said.

"Check it out yourself," I replied. And he did. The next day, he got back to me in total shock.

I apologize for not explaining either Ron's plan or my own. Ron became Interpol Secretary General two years later, so I'm fairly certain he either convinced his predecessor to fix the vulnerability or took care of it himself. But without

100% certainty, I'm not willing to jeopardize Interpol's security. Besides, the point of this story isn't to help my readers become more effective terrorists.

So what *is* the point?

To introduce another powerful tool in the failure toolbox: the pre-mortem.

We already looked at post-mortems, which help us determine the errors that led to a failure so we can do better in the future. Advocates of pre-mortems ask: why delay such an analysis until *after* a disaster? If you can anticipate danger areas in advance, you can often prevent catastrophe. By asking, "How would I blow up Interpol?" I could discover and repair security vulnerabilities before the organization's enemies could find them.

Pre-mortems can put the process of learning from failure into hyperspeed as you don't have to wait for failure to actually occur to learn from it. We saw at the end of the last chapter some of the questions you might ask when doing a post-mortem. The list would look somewhat different with pre-mortems, and might include:

1. **What are the risks that could potentially bring the project down?** Examine if there are any technical issues, resource constraints, scheduling problems or other issues to generate your list of vulnerabilities.

2. **Which of the risks identified are most likely to lead to failure?** Go though each one and identify how much it could contribute to your hypothetical project failure.

3. **For each risk, can you find a way to a) prevent it from occurring and/ or b) reduce the impact if it does occur?**

4. **Who should be in charge of each risk?** Failures don't always come from unexpected sources. Very often, we can see potential sources of failure and still not take action because we assume someone else is handling it. Clearly defining who is accountable for each risk factor can remedy that.

5. **When should we reexamine our risk factors?** Threats can increase or decrease over time. Create regular checkins or milestones ahead of time so these don't go unchecked.

Potential causes of failure are vast. As we'll see next, pre-mortem processes can differ greatly depending on whether you're addressing common or uncommon failure scenarios.

Hurry Up and Fail

The Sharks on ABC's *Shark Tank* have a reputation for driving hard bargains. Many entrepreneurs who've pitched their products on the show have been driven to tears by the Sharks' frank critiques and low valuations. Savvy presenters know how to make a solid, compelling presentation that leaves a little wiggle room for counter-offers, and Cool Jen was nothing if not savvy. She'd only started selling her product a few months earlier and already came into the Tank asking for $100,000 for a 10% share, giving her fledgeling company a million dollar valuation. She immediately got push back from the Sharks. Mr. Wonderful said her offer didn't give him enough equity to get excited about. Cool Jen told him not to worry, that she was there to negotiate.

Damon Johns started saying her valuation was nuts considering she had almost zero sales, but Mark Cuban, the billionaire owner of the Dallas Mavericks, interrupted Damon to offer Cool Jen $250,000 for a 20% share, raising her company valuation to $1,250,000, but only on condition she took his offer right away. Cool as a cucumber, Cool Jen took the deal in one of the fastest transactions in Shark Tank history.

Cool Jen is better known to the public as Jenny Goldfarb, the owner of Mrs. Goldfarb's Unreal Deli, a company that produces vegan deli meats. I'm sure she'll plotz when she reads this segment referring to her as Cool Jen, but almost a decade before she became Mrs. Goldfarb, the nickname Cool Jen had already been well earned in our household through her colorful and overly-hip vocabulary. She'd show up at our door with a "What's the dizzle?" and greet our newborn with a "What's up little dude?"

Shark Tank can skyrocket a company's sales. Each of the Sharks is a highly successful businessperson with a history of profitable product launches. Even products that don't close deals on the Tank can see sales explode following a pitch, which amounts to a free infomercial before millions of viewers. Cool Jen's launch was no exception, with her public profile and sales shooting through the roof the moment her episode aired.

But rapid growth is not without its challenges.

Take the case of Mix Bikini, another brand that successfully pitched on Shark Tank. The concept of Mix Bikini was simple. Rather than selling bikinis as sets, Mix Bikini sold tops and bottoms separately, giving customers a wider range of options. Barbara Corcoran, the real estate mogul, liked the idea and invested $50,000 for a 10% share of the company.

The night the Mix Bikini episode of *Shark Tank* aired, the company held a gigantic party, complete with open bar, swimming pool, and, of course, plenty of bikini-clad women. Barbara herself showed up and partied the night away with her latest investment.

The next day, Mix Bikini's hung-over CEO dragged himself into the office to see how many sales they made during launch night. He found none. How could millions of people learn about his company and none buy? Could *no one* have liked the idea?

Just the opposite. Women *loved* the idea. Too many women. The company's web server crashed. It hadn't been strengthened to handle the launch of a major national brand. By the time Mix Bikini brought their website back up, it was too late. They had no way to notify all those would-be customers they were back in business.

A crashed server on launch night turned out to be a disaster scenario for Mix Bikini, which literally never recovered. But the odd thing about the server crash was how predictable it was. Network Administrators regularly run their servers through what's called a stress test, which simulates the effects of a surge of traffic to see just how much of a load the server can handle.

Those who pitch on *Shark Tank* aren't always known for their ability to anticipate problems. Had Mix Bikini not gotten a deal, their failure to prepare for launch night would've been understandable. Almost. But entrepreneurs seek Sharks partially for mentorship. Barbara had already been involved in dozens of deals, so it was surprising she didn't have a team reviewing Mix Bikini's infrastructure to ensure it could handle the volume.

There's no rule that says you need to fail yourself to learn from failure. As previously discussed, the pre-mortem can be a great tool for examining a hypothetical failure before it can occur. But the process becomes even easier when dealing with actual failure scenarios that others have already faced. If someone's previously tried and crashed, it's a great shortcut to study how and why to prevent the same mistakes. In some areas, you won't just find evidence of one past disaster. There might be hundreds or even thousands of failures to learn from.

This is the situation the World Health Organization (WHO) found themselves in. Far too many patients were dying from complications during surgery. Even worse, many were entirely avoidable, involving accidents such as performing a surgery on the wrong patient or cutting open the patient's right side when the issue was on the left. When you have a vast history to learn from, you can pull out the most common causes of failure and include their lessons in your protocols. In the WHO's case, they reduced complications and fatalities from surgery by over 30% by instituting a simple one-page checklist for surgical teams to go through before each operation. The items on the checklist are all basic, such as a verbal confirmation of the patient's name, the procedure to be performed, and the location of the procedure. You'd think that information would be so fundamental the checklist would feel like a waste of time, but the thirty-plus percent improvement shows just how often these basic facts were actually missed.

Let's return to Cool Jen and Mrs. Goldfarb's Unreal Deli. If you're hoping for a dramatic climax to the story, I'm sorry to disappoint. Neither Jenny Goldfarb nor Mark Cuban had any intention of allowing Unreal Deli to become another Mix Bikini. Mark's team contacted Cool Jen and took her through their checklist of preparatory steps for launch night. They recommended having Unreal Deli on Shopify, an ecommerce platform that could handle huge spikes in traffic. Cool Jen already built her site on Shopify, so no adjustment was necessary. In the end, no server crashes or other disasters marred the excitement of Unreal Deli's launch.

Is this ending anti-climactic? For a book like this one, definitely. It's anti-climactic in the same way it's anti-climactic when an airplane arrives on schedule to its designated gate or a patient wakes up after a successful surgery. Flying a plane, going under the knife, and introducing a new product on prime-time TV are high-risk scenarios. While a completely unforeseeable crisis could happen in any of those situations, most of the problems that occur in air travel, surgery, and product launches are predictable. We can easily look back and say the Mix Bikini team should have been less concerned with throwing an epic party and more concerned with their web server strength. Similarly, we can look at a botched surgery where the surgeon operated on the wrong side of the patient and be shocked such errors can still occur.

The takeaway is simple. If you're in an area with predictable disaster scenarios, learn from past failures and use a checklist to eliminate common errors. Here are factors to take into account to build effective checklists:

1. **Identify common failure points.** Whether its your own failures or you're identifying industry-wide failures as the WHO did when creating their surgical checklist, you want to find the most common pitfalls.

2. **Weigh the cost of including an item on your checklist vs leaving it off.** The point of the checklist is not to create more bureaucracy. The longer the list, the more inefficiency it can create. It's worth becoming less efficient to avoid an airplane crash, but if your cost of failure is low, you may opt for a shorter list with only very common problems included.

3. **Build your list in the correct sequence.** The items on the list should be logically organized, usually following the order of operations.

4. **Keep it simple.** The meaning of each item on the checklist should be obvious to everyone. Avoid jargon, acronyms, or technical terms that might confuse team members.

Checklists are fairly straightforward ways of avoiding common problems. But what do you do when the disaster scenarios are less predictable and a basic checklist is insufficient preparation?

On May 12, 2013, Chris Hadfield played David Bowie's *Space Oddity* in what Bowie called "possibly the most poignant version of the song ever created." What made the rendition so powerful? It wasn't his voice or guitar playing, both of which are fine but hardly at superstar levels. The recording was unique was because it took place 220 miles above the earth's surface while moving at 17,000 miles per hour aboard the International Space Station (ISS).

Chris's first voyage into space was aboard the Space Shuttle Atlantis, which was scheduled to dock with the Russian space station Mir on November 15, 1995. A decade prior, such a docking would have been inconceivable. Back then, the United States and the Soviet Union were in the thick of the Cold War, and each one closely guarded their military and space technology. However, in 1991, the Soviet Union collapsed. The US worried advanced Soviet technology could be abandoned, or even worse, fall into unfriendly hands. So the United States drastically shifted policy to cooperate with the Russian Space Agency, even provided funding for important projects.

Before Chris's mission, a US shuttle had docked with the Mir Space Station once before, but the docking was hacked and awkward. This time, the Atlantis had flown into orbit carrying a five-ton, fifteen-foot-long docking module. Their mission was to permanently affix the docking module to Mir so all future shuttles could easily link up with the Russian station. Docking in space isn't easy under the best of circumstances. In this case, the Atlantis had a 15-foot tower sticking out of the shuttle blocking their vision and a docking window of only two minutes. Of course, having the tower jutting into space and the short docking window was part of the plan. Having broken sensors was not.

In the previous chapter, we learned about two flights, Ethiopian Airlines Flight ET302 and Lion Air Flight JT610, that crashed when faulty sensors fed their computers incorrect data. Those were just routine flights. This was a US Shuttle and a Russian space station docking together for only the second time in history, anything but routine. As they approached, one of the laser sensors on the shuttle told Chris the shuttle was 32 feet away from Mir. But a second laser sensor told him the shuttle was only 20 feet away. A 12-foot difference is enormous. If the shuttle accidentally attempted to dock 12 feet into the Mir, the two would crash. The Mir would depressurize, killing everyone aboard, and the shuttle could sustain enough damage to burn up upon reentry to the atmosphere.

Fortunately, Chris had been preparing for this moment his entire life. He was 9-years-old when Neil Armstrong walked on the moon, and, like millions of other kids watching, Chris wanted to become an astronaut. At the time, he could see no clear path to ever achieving his goal. The space race between the United States and the Soviets didn't include Canadians like himself, and it was hard to perceive Canada ever competing on that stage.

Of course, Neil Armstrong also couldn't have foreseen a realistic path to walking on the moon when he was nine but still did it 29 years later. So the 9-year-old Chris Hadfield decided not to let realism get in the way. Without telling anyone his goal, he made changes to start living like an astronaut and be prepared when opportunity struck. If he woke up tired and sluggish, he'd ask himself, "Would an astronaut roll over and go back to sleep or would he force himself to get up?"

For decades, Chris made choices with an eye toward space, becoming both an engineer and a test pilot. And when NASA finally came knocking, he was ready.

By the time Chris pulled out his guitar to show the world how music functions in space, he'd already spent over 160 days off-planet during three journeys, most notably as commander of the ISS. But despite spending more time in space than only a handful of humans, Chris is quick to note only a tiny percent of his actions as an astronaut took place in orbit.

So what did he do with the rest of his time?

It was divided between providing support for other missions and enormous amounts of training. Moments in space are precious and extremely expensive. NASA doesn't want astronauts fumbling around and wasting valuable time in orbit, so every task they perform in space is first done over and over on the ground to ensure maximum efficiency.

But it's not just the foreseeable challenges of space they drill. NASA and its partner space agencies are obsessed with a very specific type of pre-mortems: simulations. They simulate disaster after disaster that might occur in space. And many of them actually do.

Let's go back to the 737 Max crashes for a second. Both planes had sensor failures. The pilots surely knew such errors could happen, but the

Lion Air pilots didn't know a sensor failure could trigger a secret software program to nosedive their plane. The Ethiopian Airlines pilots knew about the software, but didn't know they'd only have ten seconds to fix it. And none of the pilots had spent *any* time in flight simulators practicing for this scenario.

When Atlantis went to dock with Mir, the stakes were extremely high and the margin of error exceedingly small. Fortunately, the Atlantis crew had drilled this docking repeatedly. And they hadn't just drilled docking under ideal circumstances. Their simulations involved dozens of scenarios of what could go wrong, and the crew drilled those as well.

The disaster scenarios included sensors returning incorrect data. In fact, Chris created a cheat sheet for himself with distance vs time. Using that cheat sheet, a view from a camera at the back of the shuttle, and the second hand on his wristwatch, Chris was prepared to eyeball the approach and dock without guidance from the sensors.

The result? Chris judged the actual distance to be about 22 feet away. He and the other crew on deck coordinated the approach using their watches and eyes. In the end, they docked at the correct speed, coming in only three seconds early. But as often happens in space, they resolved one problem only to confront another. The shuttle successfully connected, but its latch wouldn't open; it was sealed too tight. To overcome that obstacle, Chris used a non-space age solution. He pulled out a Swiss Army Knife and cut his way through.

This is neither my first nor last anecdote involving NASA. Is this because I'm some sort of space nerd? No, it's because this is a book about failure. I don't say that as a criticism of NASA, but as a recognition of the amount that can go wrong in space. The space agency has had its share of spectacular failures (and we'll look at one a little later), but for every one of its actual failures, NASA's successfully averted hundreds more.

NASA is obsessive about its simulations. They built a 6.2 million gallon swimming pool (about ten times the volume of an Olympic swimming pool) called the Neutral Buoyancy Laboratory to simulate a zero gravity environment. If a mission requires a spacewalk, they'll drill it repeatedly in the pool.

Simulations help space agencies discover problems on the ground before encountering them under the harsh conditions of outer space. For instance, in one ISS simulation, run by the Russian team, they filled a practice capsule with so much smoke that by the time the crew got their gas masks on, they could no longer see their feet. Chris, acting according to American protocols, evacuated the crew to a part of the station sealed off from the smoked-in module where they could regroup and form a plan. But the Russians weren't pleased with this response. They'd been trained to stay and fight a fire, to prioritize saving the lab over the crew. The simulation helped both teams identify a gap in culture and formulate a plan for handling such a scenario in the future.

Chris has died over and over again during these simulations. Most of the time, his death came about because of a poor response to a simulated disaster. But on at least one occasion, his death *was* the simulation. It started with a report that he was injured in space. The crew had to determine how to handle a severely injured astronaut. But before they'd gotten much farther, more bad news came in: Chris had died of his injuries.

At this point, the crew had to deal with a wide range of questions. What should they do with the corpse? There were no body bags on the ISS. Should they store it in a space suit? And what about its long-term resting place? Would they return the body to earth for a proper burial? Should they let it float off into space? Or should they hold a ceremonial cremation with the body burning up when it reentered the atmosphere?

Someone also needed to get in touch with Chris's family. Should they deliver the news over the phone or in person? Before they could make any decisions, the scenario got worse. The press got wind of a disaster in space. How should they handle the PR? And who would take the lead, NASA or the Canadian Space Agency?

Chris's wife had been planning to go trekking in the Himalayas during his long stint in space. After running through the simulation, she realized that should anything go wrong, she didn't want to be on the other side of the world with limited communication and no way to quickly return home. In the end, she postponed her Himalayan adventure and went hiking in Utah instead.

Simulations can be resource intensive, but they can be fabulous tools for finding and fixing potential problems before they arise. Let's look at a few components that can play into a successful simulation:

1. **Identify a clear objective.** Determine exactly what you're hoping to achieve with the simulation. Are you hoping to identify bottlenecks? Test your process under load? Make sure all systems work as expected?

2. **Plan your scenarios.** Outline a range of scenarios that might arise, including one everything goes right, some with minor issues, and some with major issues so you can see how your team and system handle each situation.

3. **Create a realistic environment.** The simulation should mimic the real-world environment as closely as possible, especially in the area you're testing. For NASA, they'll simulate spacewalks in a pool. What do you need to simulate and how can you make it as realistic as possible?

4. **Clarify roles and responsibilities.** Each participant in the simulation should have a clearly defined role that mirrors the role they'll play in real life. This will ensure that everyone knows what they need to do and can help identify gaps or overlaps in responsibilities.

5. **Define your success metrics.** That which is measured tends to improve. Figure out what metrics would be most useful to measure the success of your simulation. Is it the time it takes to resolve issues? The amount of user engagement? Revenue? You want to go in knowing your key performance indicators so you can see where you need to improve.

6. **Test under stress.** Push your systems and team to their limits to see how they handle high-pressure situations. This can help identify weaknesses that might not be visible under normal conditions.

7. **Gather feedback.** After the simulation, poll the participants and analyze the data. What went well? What didn't? Did any unexpected issues arise?

8. **Pinpoint actionable insights.** The simulation is only as valuable as the takeaways you derive from it. What concrete changes should you make based on the simulation results? Do you have any systems that need to be upgraded? Does your team need additional training?

Understanding what could go wrong and planning your reactions in advance can enable you to make better, faster decisions if problems arise. While Chris Hadfield commanded the ISS, the fire alarm did actually go off. Fires in space are extremely dangerous, but no one panicked because the entire crew had drilled onboard fires. They calmly conducted checks until they found the root of the problem, which was merely a broken smoke detector. But had it been something more serious, they had the training and presence of mind to react.

Hurry Up and Fail

The original version of David Bowie's *Space Oddity* ends with Major Tom floating helplessly in space after losing communication with Earth.

> *Ground Control to Major Tom*
> *Your circuit's dead,*
> *there's something wrong*

Meanwhile, Tom sings…

> *Here am I floating*
> *round my tin can*
> *Far above the Moon*
> *Planet Earth is blue*
> *And there's nothing I can do.*

Chris recorded his version immediately before returning to Earth following a five-month stint on the ISS. He changed the ending as follows:

> *Ground Control to Major Tom*
> *The time is near, there's not too long*

While Chris sings:

> *Here am I floating in my tin can*
> *Last glimpse of the world*
> *Planet Earth is blue*
> *And there's nothing left to do*

All Chris Hadfield's years of training paid off. By preparing himself for the worst, he avoided the worst, and his simulated death in space was never repeated in reality.

Unlike checklists, simulations aren't cheap or easy to pull off, but they can effectively prepare you against potential causes of disaster.

How well do you learn from failure?
Take the Failure Scorecard at
DaveMasonAuthor.com/failure-scorecard

PART 4

Mitigating Failure

CHAPTER 10

Protect Your Downside

"Failure is the opportunity to grow, to learn, to reassess and come back even stronger."

- RICHARD BRANSON

In 1991, Richard Branson and Per Lindstrand set out to make history. Again. In 1987, the pair had completed the longest balloon flight of all time when they flew over the Atlantic ocean. Four years later, they hoped to eclipse their own record by flying over the far wider Pacific.

To survive the altitude, the two men wouldn't travel in a basket as in a traditional balloon flight, but in a pressurized capsule. Immediately before the trip, Per confessed to Richard that he hadn't tested the capsule in a pressure chamber, so he couldn't be 100% sure it would stay intact at 40,000 feet. Per said, "If the capsule decompresses, you'll notice that it suddenly becomes misty. The capsule will appear to fill with fog. You will hear a screaming in your ears and you will experience the sensation of your lungs being sucked out of your chest and through your mouth."

To say record-breaking hot air balloon flights are dangerous would be a gigantic understatement. Before Branson and Per completed their transatlantic flight, seven others had tried and failed. Five died in the attempt. Per almost died in their Atlantic crossing, surviving only after treading water for two hours without a life jacket.

While Branson and Per waited for the winds to strengthen for their Pacific crossing, Japanese balloonist Fumio Niwa launched first, hoping to beat them to the punch. Fumio only made it 10 miles into the 8000 mile journey when his balloon fell apart, and he was forced to ditch into the ocean. By the time a rescue helicopter reached him, Fumio was dead.

On January 15, 1991, Branson and Per finally launched. The balloon carried six fuel tanks, and their plan was to jettison empty tanks into the ocean to decrease weight. But when the pair attempted to jettison the first empty tank, two full ones went with it.

This created two problems. Long term, they lacked sufficient fuel for their intended flight path, leaving them with a high probability of crashing somewhere in the middle of the Pacific. But they had a more immediate problem. They had dropped so much weight that the balloon shot up like a rocket. The glass dome of their capsule would likely explode once they reached 43,000 feet. Should their balloon become depressurized at that height, they'd have about two seconds to live, just enough time to feel their eyeballs get sucked out of their sockets.

Fortunately, Branson and Per had dropped to 25,000 feet to jettison the tank, which gave them a bit of cushion, but not much. In no time, they'd reached 38,000 feet. They opened the top of the balloon to let out hot air, but the balloon continued to rise, hitting 42,000 feet and still going. Finally, at 42,500 feet, the altimeter flattened out.

Having averted immediate death, they turned their attention on surviving the next few days. They considered dropping the balloon in the ocean, but high seas made an ocean rescue impossible. To cross the Pacific with just three remaining fuel tanks, they'd need to average 170 miles per hour, twice the speed any balloon had reached before. They could only reach those speeds by riding the center of the jet stream, a vein of wind only a hundred meters wide, about four times the width of the balloon itself.

Despite being a self-proclaimed atheist, in his first autobiography, aptly titled *Losing my Virginity*, Richard Branson recalls sensing a spirit had entered the capsule and was helping him along, somehow helping the balloon stay within this tiny vein of crazy fast air to propel it forward at speeds reaching 240 miles per hour.

Then the capsule caught fire.

To block the fire from destroying the balloon, they rose back to heights where oxygen levels are so low that fire can't burn, even though that required them to approach the 43,000 foot altitude where they risked an explosion.

How many near death experiences have we already tallied on this flight? Three? They had at least one more coming: a crash landing on a frozen lake in Canada in the middle of a blizzard, where they almost died from exposure before they could be rescued.

Protect Your Downside

This long list of nearly fatal instances does not indicate a particularly unlucky flight. To the contrary, we just recounted one of Branson's most *successful* balloon flights. The events of his unsuccessful flights are even more catastrophic, including landing in the middle of a civil war and nearly being shot down by hostile countries who hadn't given him permission to fly over their airspace.

And his insane, record-breaking attempts are not limited to ballooning. The *Virgin Atlantic Challenger* sank to the bottom of the ocean while trying to break the record for the fastest Atlantic crossing by a surface vessel. Undeterred, Branson tried again with *Virgin Atlantic Challenger II*, and this time succeeded in breaking a speed record that had stood for 34 years.

Next to the brazenness of the billionaire's feats, Everest expeditions are routine and safe. As much as the public falls in love with daredevils, the sad truth is risk-takers like Richard Branson rarely live long. It's even more rare for them to build stable, successful companies. But that's just what Branson's done. And not just once, but over 400 times!

So how has he managed it?

Some of Branson's success is no doubt due to his larger-than-life personality. His exploits have earned his companies billions of dollars in free publicity.

Imagine you were launching a new soda company in the United States. What would you do to alert the media? You'd certainly send out a press release. You'd likely have a kickoff party. Maybe throw in a ribbon cutting or feature a few high-profile celebrities drinking your soda. When launching Virgin Cola in the US, Branson drove a Sherman Tank through New York's Times Square. The tank plowed through a wall of cola cans and then fired a shot, causing a Coke billboard to explode (or appear to explode, an illusion created by fireworks). In other exploits, Branson bungee jumped off the 407 foot tall Palms Hotel Casino in Las Vegas for the first Virgin America flight, and he wore a wedding dress and shaved his signature beard for the launch of Virgin Brides.

But not all of his stunts have been so frivolous. Virgin Atlantic was still in its infancy in 1990 during the months leading up to the Gulf War. Branson grew concerned about the state of the foreign nationals stranded in Bagdad, so he used his political connections to strike a deal with Saddam Hussein and flew one of his four planes into Bagdad on a rescue mission. One gets the sense in his autobiography that the press he received was almost a source of embarrassment, as this flight wasn't a mere publicity stunt, it was a way to help those in genuine need.

But if you only see Branson as a larger-than-life, publicity seeking daredevil who built wealth by keeping his face in the paper, you'll miss a core element of his success. That would be a shame, because it's not easy to duplicate Branson's stature as a media darling, and it's nearly impossible to live his daredevil life and outpace death. But when you unpack the secrets of Branson's business success, you'll find a different lesson buried beneath all the glitter.

Let's take a deeper look at Branson's remarkable success story, focusing on just the fundamentals without the antics.

Branson dropped out of high school at age fifteen to launch a magazine that campaigned against the war in Vietnam and gave voice to his generation. Dropping out of school to start a business venture is unusual enough. But when you're dyslexic and your business idea involves launching a magazine, it sounds downright screwy.

But Branson believed in trial by fire. "The best way of running a business is just to throw yourself in the deep end and learn all those things and ask lots of questions. Listen, listen, listen. And that's what I did when I was young."

It's now been over 50 years since he launched *Student* and while few would still call Richard Branson screwy, a whole host of other labels have stuck. He's now Sir Richard Branson, the eccentric, audacious, outlandish, innovative billionaire founder of more than 400 companies. Amongst these descriptions, you'll rarely hear words such as cautious or calculating, but you should.

Branson may have dropped out of high school, but he didn't do it rashly. His father made him a deal: he could drop out of school to start his magazine only after he covered the printing costs of the first edition. Branson went to work calling companies, pitching them on advertising slots for his new magazine. Only once he raised the 4000 pounds for the paper and printing did he publish. By then, there was zero risk as each sale was profit. Branson continued with this strategy on future editions, only printing once advertisers had already covered his costs.

Of course, this strategy is a lot easier to pull off with a magazine than with an airline, right? After all, you can't wait to buy your planes until you've sold enough tickets to cover costs. Not quite, but Branson pulled off something almost as good.

Starting an airline is a high-risk proposition. Margins are notoriously slim and high-profile bankruptcies are more the norm than the exception. Branson's big, early success came with Virgin Records. He'd spent 20 years building it into one of the hottest independent labels in the world, and profits were at an all time high. His partners and investors were less than thrilled when Branson announced he wanted to leverage that success to start an airline to compete with British Airways. Success building a record label hardly showed competence in the airline industry.

But Branson had learned his lesson well with the founding of *Student* Magazine. Raising printing costs before going to press minimized risk. Even post-launch, Branson continued to be a master of keeping costs low. For much of its existence, the magazine ran out of a church crypt with his desk nothing more than a marble slab spread across two tombs. The reason for this morbid office suite? The pastor lent him the crypt for free.

With his heart set on starting Virgin Atlantic, Branson entered negotiations with Boeing for the purchase of a second-hand 747. He was an outsider to the airline industry, but if Boeing thought this brash young entrepreneur was going to be a pushover, they were sorely mistaken. As Branson says, "If you are a risk taker, then the art is to protect the downside." Branson offered to buy the plane on one condition, that he could return it to Boeing at the end of the first year should Virgin Atlantic fail.

Needless to say, Boeing didn't like this idea. Nordstrom might allow you to return a sweater, but aircraft manufacturers aren't in the habit of offering refunds. A 747 is an expensive purchase. Boeing wanted the plane off their books and the sale finalized. They didn't want the risk it might come back in a year's time.

But Branson had leverage. Aircraft sales were down, and Boeing had a particular interest in seeing a competitor rise against British Airways. In the end, not only did Boeing agree to give Branson his money back should his airline flop, they agreed that if plane prices went up in the interim, they'd refund him *more* than he paid. Someone at Boeing quipped, "It's easier to sell a fleet of jumbos to an American airline than just one to Virgin."

Protecting the downside has indeed been one of Virgin Group's core philosophies. This, perhaps more than any other factor, has allowed Virgin to expand into so many arenas. Normally businesses stay within a narrow area of expertise, but Virgin's companies are all over the map. Beyond music, air flight, and cola, they've ventured into banking, mobile phones, space tourism, and much more.

It's important to note not all these businesses have been successful. Virgin Cola enjoyed tremendous early success but ultimately got out-muscled by Coke, which forced enough stores to stop carrying the upstart rival that it went out of business. Yet, none of the failures ever threaten to destroy Virgin Group as a whole because of Branson's obsession with protecting the downside.

How does Virgin manage downside protection across such a wide range of businesses? Let me present just a few elements in their risk minimization formula.

First, it's important to understand Virgin is not a single company with a range of products. Rather, the Virgin Group owns and operates a collection of companies. While Virgin Cola was no doubt served onboard Virgin Atlantic flights, each one functioned independently. This business structure greatly limits the downside of a failure. Indeed, Virgin Atlantic, after decades of success, filed for bankruptcy protection after COVID-19 forced it, and virtually every other airline, to massively cut flights. But Virgin Mobile was spared sharing the airline's fate because the two ventures are not part of the same corporation.

Another key ingredient to minimizing their downside is their preference for partnerships. Rather than owning 100% of a business, Virgin Group prefers to start new businesses in partnership with industry insiders. Virgin brings their extraordinary brand and culture to the deal, their partners bring expertise in the specific business area, and they jointly form a new corporation.

What Branson refers to as protecting your downside, I refer to as Asymmetrical Risk/Reward, a concept Chana and I teach in greater depth in our novel *The Size of Your Dreams*. The concept is simple, even if the execution isn't always. Whenever possible, risk little to gain much.

By only printing once he had his costs covered, Branson's magazine became a low-risk, high-reward venture. By having a money-back guarantee on his first airplane, Branson made his airline, which would normally be a high-risk venture, into a much lower risk one.

As you get ready to launch your next project, stop and ask yourself, "How can I protect my downside?" In other words, how can you minimize the risk so that even if you fail, you'll lose little, but if you succeed, you'll still win big? The following steps can help:

1. **Identify all potential risks.** The risk you haven't considered is a bigger threat than the one's you've already weighed. Make a list of all risks and their likelihood to block your success.

2. **Attempt to mitigate each risk.** For each one, see if there's a way you can protect the downside, such as how Branson did by raising the money to print *Student* magazine first.

3. **Make sure failures can't cause chain reactions.** By making each of his ventures an independent corporation, Branson didn't jeopardize healthy companies when others failed. So too, you can put legal and financial protections in place to stop one failure from bringing down your entire operation.

4. **Negotiate away risk.** As we saw in Chapter 5, there is huge upside and little downside from asking for what you want, and you can use this technique to remove risk factors. Branson knew he had a huge risk of failing with his airline, and he knew Boeing badly wanted to sell him a 747. So he negotiated that he could return the plane if he failed.

5. **Follow clear patterns of success.** Branson formed partnerships with industry insiders when penetrating new markets. While you don't necessarily need partnerships, you can model your efforts on those that have already been successful for others.

6. **Create early warning systems.** The sooner you learn of problems, the less likely they are to derail you. This is such an important factor that all of the next chapter is devoted to exploring it in depth.

CHAPTER 11

Build Early Warning Systems

"Failures are finger posts on the road to achievement."

- C.S. Lewis

In 2016, Buenos Aires hosted the Time Warp Festival, a techno and house music festival started in Mannheim, Germany during the mid-90's raving craze. It featured top underground DJs, blaring music, flashing lights, insane dancing, and, of course, plenty of drugs.

But in Buenos Aires in 2016, something went wrong. On the first night, a bad batch of drugs circulated, leaving six participants dead. The rest of the festival was canceled, the event organizers were arrested, the mayor of Buenos Aires banned all future music festivals, and a judge banned "all commercial activity and live and recorded music" in the city.

In neighboring Uruguay, the Time Warp deaths also shook up the locals. With their own electronic music festival, La Terraza, just a few months away, how could they prevent a Time Warp tragedy on their own soil?

They had several options. They could have followed the Buenos Aires model and simply canceled the festival. Alternatively, they could have done extensive security searches of each ticket-holder. Drugs are part of Rave culture, and searches could have ferreted out huge amounts of illegal drugs, leading to dozens of arrests. But searches and arrests would have ruined the festival's vibe.

Instead, they ran drug tests.

When I think of drug tests, my mind goes first to sports, where random screenings curb the use of performance-enhancing drugs. Employers also do drug testing to assure applicants and staff are sober. But the tests launched in Uruguay for La Terraza were of a different sort entirely. They weren't performed on individuals to keep them drug-free. Instead, they tested *drugs themselves* to catch adulterations.

The Uruguay approach was a radical departure from standard drug control measures. Rather than increasing police presence and stepping up arrests, Uruguay accepted drug use as inevitable and tried to make it safer.

During the La Terraza festival, drug testers carried out 135 tests on LSD, ketamine, and cocaine. In five instances, tests revealed potentially dangerous adulterants, including a sample of cocaine found to be laced with the anti-parasitic Levamisole.

A batch of 135 drug tests at a large music festival like La Terraza is only a drop in the bucket. Drug users were wary of bringing their stash into testing tents, and the vast majority skipped the option despite measures to create an atmosphere of trust such as keeping the drug tests anonymous and protecting drug users from legal consequences.

Indeed, such a solution may seem naive. With tens of thousands at a festival, how much impact could 135 drug tests make? For each dose tested, a hundred likely eluded the testers. If the point was to find and remove tainted drugs from the festival, we would have to consider the effort a failure. However, that wasn't the point of the testing. So what was?

The creation of an early warning system.

The drugs at Time Warp didn't have a 100% fatality rate. Six died, but others took critically ill. Presumably, many more were exposed to the same batch of drugs without severe consequences, either because they took lower doses or had stronger tolerance for the adulterants.

Imagine the Time Warp festival again, but now with La Terraza style testing tents. The vast majority of drug carriers would walk past the tents without entering, but a small percent would have taken the offer. Given the wide circulation of an adulterated drug and the symptoms experienced by those taking it, odds are that before long, testers would sample a dose with the dangerous adulterant. Since the festival wished to create a safe environment rather than stamp out all drug use, the DJs could have announced the discovery and warned participants.

At this point, many more who purchased that drug would likely proceed to the testing tents to make sure they weren't at risk. As testers found more adulterated samples, they could have notified hospitals, had emergency medical

Build Early Warning Systems

teams sent to the scene, and perhaps even tracked down the dealer. Further announcements could have warned participants of symptoms to be on the lookout for and encouraged anyone experiencing such symptoms to seek help. If the situation continued to worsen, the festival itself could then be cancelled, but more likely, such precautions would have averted a disaster.

Early warning systems can be critical to minimizing the downside of your failures. Let's look at a few factors for effectively creating early warning systems:

1. **Identify potential risks.** It's far easier to create an early warning system around a specific risk, so brainstorm in advance all the risks you want to build warning systems around. In La Terraza, they focused on just one, adulterated drugs, but you may have multiple risks you wish to account for.

2. **Define Key Risk Indicators (KRIs).** Many business talk about KPIs, Key Performance Indicators, but it's just as important to know which metrics in your business can signal that a risky situation is developing. KRIs can include customer satisfaction scores, downtime frequency, or specific financial ratios. The important thing is that KRIs be actionable, measurable, and directly tied to the risk you hope to mitigate.

3. **Establish thresholds.** For each KRI, determine the threshold that could signal a crisis. In the early days of my ecommerce business, if I hadn't received a single sale by 9am, I'd take a quick look to make sure the website was functioning. If nothing came in by 10am, I'd do a deeper inspection of the shopping cart. Some days just started slow, so this KRI didn't always indicate a problem, but it was a dependable rule of thumb for when to increase my vigilance.

4. **Plan your response.** How will you react if the KRI threshold is crossed? Who is responsible for responding? How will that person be notified there's a potential problem? Is there a clear plan for how to investigate the issue? For escalating the response if a legitimate problem is discovered?

An early warning system can greatly reduce the negative impact of our failures. But as we'll see in the next chapter, there is one big caveat. You must actually heed the warnings.

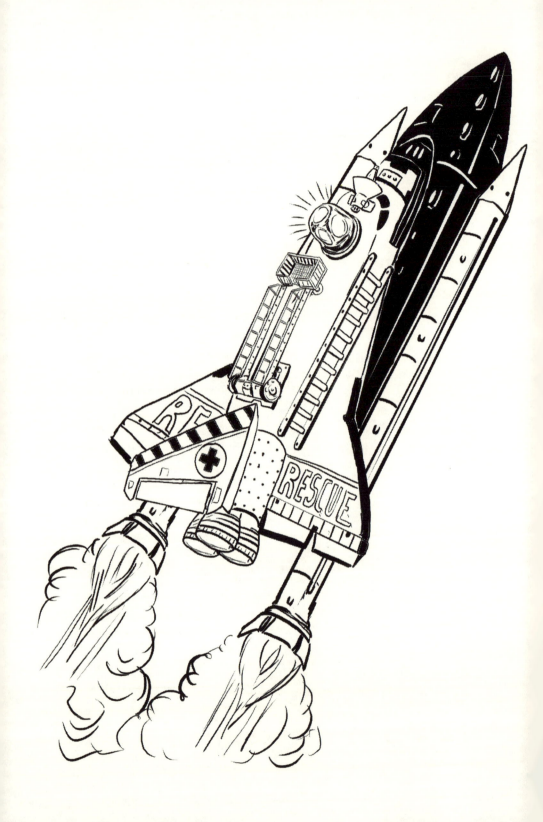

CHAPTER 12

Heed the Signs

"Failure is the best teacher, but not everyone wants to go to his class."

- UNKNOWN

A few years ago, our family attempted to explore the Ramon Crater in southern Israel. This natural formation is one of the largest craters in the world, formed by millions of years of erosion. Not only does it offer extensive hiking, but the crater is renowned for fantastic stargazing. Unfortunately, our timing was horrible for both hiking and stargazing. Rain is rare in the Negev desert, but we arrived right in the middle of a storm, and visibility was so poor that even from the shelter of the visitor's center, we couldn't see into the famous crater only a few feet away.

With hiking out of the question, we explored the visitor's center's indoor options, which included exhibits on the history, geology, flora, and fauna of the Ramon Crater. But then we saw another exhibit we weren't expecting: a memorial museum dedicated to an entirely different Ramon, Ilan Ramon, the most famous pilot in Israeli history.

Born Ilan Wolferman on June 20, 1954, just six years after Israel achieved independence, Ilan's personal history closely models that of the young country into which he was born. His father, Eliezer, escaped Nazi Germany in 1935. His mother, originally Polish, survived the Auschwitz concentration camp before making it to Israel in 1949. When Ilan joined the Israeli Air Force, he exchanged his European last name for a more Israeli one, Ramon.

Ilan fought in two of Israel's wars, the Yom Kippur War in 1973 and the Lebanon War in 1982, but his most impactful mission for the Israeli Air Force wasn't flown during wartime. In fact, it was flown against the protests of many of the country's top military and political figures who considered it a foolhardy move with potentially catastrophic consequences.

On June 7, 1981, Ilan Ramon and seven other pilots took off from Sinai's Etzion Airbase in heavily armed F-16s. Since midair refueling would be impossible, each plane was equipped with an external fuel tank so they'd have enough gas to return to Israel. But even with the extra fuel, it was considered a longshot that the pilots would make it back alive.

A near-critical mistake occurred soon after takeoff when the jets flew over the yacht of Jordan's King Hussein while passing the Red Sea. King Hussein identified the Israeli planes and astutely guessed their target. But Ramon and company experienced their first bit of luck when the King's warning to his allies never got through. The Israeli pilots conversed with one another in Arabic, pretending to be Saudi while flying over Jordan and Jordanian while flying over Saudi Arabia.

The Israelis knew Iraq was confident no attack would ever come from Saudi Arabia and thus had a blind spot on their radar along their Saudi border. So the team flew right through it. As they approached their target, Osirak nuclear reactor, the Israelis experienced their second piece of luck. A half-hour before arrival, the Iraqi soldiers manning the reactor's anti-aircraft defense left their post for an afternoon meal and turned off their radar. At least eight Israeli bombs struck the reactor, which at the time contained 13 kilograms of uranium enriched to 93%, nearly enough to create a nuclear bomb.

International criticism was fierce in the wake of the Osirak bombing, but Israel's actions were viewed in a new light a decade later, after the Iraqi invasion of Kuwait. One can only speculate how history would have played out if Saddam Hussein had succeeded in creating his nuclear arsenal.

But Ilan Ramon's international fame came on an entirely different stage. Twenty-two years later, on January 16, 2003, Ramon took off on his most famous flight. This time, his ship carried no weapons and fought no enemy. The purpose of this flight was to build international cooperation and conduct research that could benefit the entire world. During the 16-day mission, the crew conducted over 75 scientific experiments. But the Ilan Ramon memorial at the Ramon Crater wasn't built to honor the scientific advancements made during the flight. It exists because neither Ilan Ramon nor any of his six crew mates ever returned alive.

Heed the Signs

For years, I struggled to understand the concept of escape velocity, the speed needed for objects to enter orbit, approximately 7.9 kilometers per second, over 20 times the speed of sound. This is so fast that orbiting objects like the International Space Station rotate the Earth approximately once every 90 minutes.

In retrospect, my failure to grasp escape velocity probably originated with all the footage I'd seen of astronauts floating in space. I'd become so used to the concept that space was a zero-gravity environment that I couldn't understand why rockets had to travel so fast once they'd already reached space. Since there was no gravity pulling against them, why couldn't they simply use less power and orbit at a slower speed?

I should have known better from personal experience. I grew up along the water and saw from an early age that the most extreme tides coincided with full or new moons. Later, I learned every tide was caused by the impact of the moon's gravitational force on our oceans. So if the moon, which is almost 240,000 miles away and has only about 1.2 percent of Earth's mass, still exerts enough gravitational force to create the tides, then how can astronauts in orbit, who rarely go beyond 300 miles from Earth's surface, possibly escape its gravity?

The answer, of course, is they can't. Astronauts in orbit only escape about 10% of Earth's gravity. So if they still feel 90% of the gravitational pull, why aren't they pulled right back down? The answer is speed. Once an object hits escape velocity, gravity can't pull it down to Earth before it's moved far enough sideways that it misses the planet. The combination of the downward pull of gravity and the sideways speed of escape velocity instead causes objects to spin around the planet in an orbit.

The challenge with taking a spacecraft to escape velocity is that to return it to Earth in one piece, you need to slow it back down. Space is essentially frictionless, so orbiting objects can move without creating heat or using significant energy to maintain speed. But reentry is a different story. As soon as an orbiting object hits the atmosphere, it meets massive resistance. This is effective at slowing the object, but it also generates tremendous heat.

Satellites can't withstand the strains of reentry and most simply burn up in the atmosphere. But when sending humans into space, we can't allow them to combust on reentry. To ensure a safe return, all human-bearing spaceships since the dawn of the space age have been equipped with heat shields.

On January 16, 2003, the space shuttle Columbia launched into space for the 28th and last time, carrying Ilan Ramon and six other astronauts. 82 seconds after liftoff, a piece of foam fell off an external fuel tank attached to the shuttle. Foam might not sound like a highly dangerous object, but it's estimated the foam struck the left wing of the space shuttle at approximately 500 miles per hour.

Hurry Up and Fail

To be fair, at the time of the launch, no one realized a two-foot-long chunk of foam struck the Columbia. But NASA had excellent early warning systems in place. Just one day later, a team reviewed the footage in super slow motion and discovered the foam strike. NASA's Debris Assessment Team mathematically modeled the collision to see if it was severe enough to cause a problem, but their review was inconclusive.

If you were NASA at this point, what would you do? You know a two-foot-chunk of foam struck a heat-resistant tile on the wing at approximately 500 miles per hour, but you don't know whether or not it caused damage. What would be your next step?

If it were me, the first thing I'd want to know is whether any of the highly sensitive, heat-resistant tiles were damaged during the foam strike. It turns out NASA had two ways to assess whether Columbia sustained significant damage. An astronaut could have performed a spacewalk to investigate the wing, or images of the wing could have been taken by a nearby satellite. At least three requests were submitted within NASA to have such images taken. The requests were denied on the grounds that they were unnecessary and thus a waste of time. A full week passed before the crew was even informed of the problem, but even then it was only to prepare them to answer questions for the media, not for damage assessment.

I'm sure you know by now how the story ends. No assessment was ever done. The foam strike apparently broke a heat-resistant tile, causing a hole in the shuttle's only defense against the 3000-degree Fahrenheit temperatures (1650° Celsius) that built up in front of the reentering shuttle. That oversight caused Columbia to break apart 40 miles above land. Searchers later recovered over 84,000 pieces of debris spread across Texas and southern Louisiana.

But even if the damaged heat tile had been discovered prior to reentry, could anything have been done to avert the disaster? Repairing the heat-resistant tile was out of the question. The investigation board concluded there was no way the Columbia crew could have repaired the broken tile in space. However, there was another option: a space rescue.

The astronauts on Columbia were relatively safe while they remained in space, at least for a short time. The biggest concern of an extended mission would not have been running out of oxygen, food, or water. It would have been the buildup of carbon dioxide. Humans exhale carbon dioxide with each breath, and if carbon dioxide levels get too high, breathing can be fatal.

The unavoidable carbon dioxide buildup gave NASA a rescue window before Columbia's air quality became fatal. The question was, did they have a large enough time to get another shuttle into space to perform the rescue before the astronauts died?

Had they discovered the damage and attempted the rescue, NASA would have found their timing extraordinarily lucky. From 1999 through 2002, NASA conducted 19 shuttle launches, averaging just over one launch every two months. But the shuttle Atlantis was scheduled to launch on March 1, 2003, just four weeks after Columbia was due to return.

A shuttle launch is a long process, involving literally millions of steps. To get Atlantis into space in time to rescue the Columbia astronauts, two things would have had to happen.

First, NASA would have needed to put the Atlantis launch process into overdrive, scrapping any non-essential steps to get the shuttle into orbit as fast as possible. Meanwhile, they would place Columbia into low power mode so life support systems could function longer. Like the shuttle itself, the astronauts would also minimize all motion and activity to slow their breathing, and thus their creation of carbon dioxide.

Earlier in the book, we talked about Andy Weir's extraordinary novel *The Martian*, which featured NASA's attempt to rescue an astronaut stranded on Mars. One element the book emphasizes repeatedly is how much effort humanity will expend to save even a single life.

To create public policy, there are models that estimate the value of a human life. Want to raise the speed limit in a certain area? We'll weigh the increased efficiency against the number of additional deaths we estimate will result from car accidents. The same principle applies to environmental regulations. Strengthen air pollution regulations and fewer people will die from respiratory conditions, but compliance will cause businesses to lose profits. So how much is a human life worth? According to these models, approximately $10 million.

In *The Martian*, the total cost of bringing Mark Watney home alive probably totaled billions of dollars. But that cost didn't come across as unrealistic in the novel, because the $10 million figure is only for a statistical life. Statistical lives are nameless and faceless. But that number goes out the window when a *specific* human life is at risk. When a single child is trapped down a well, people mobilize from around the world to help with the rescue.

In 1970, when Apollo 13 suffered a critical failure that put the lives of its crew in jeopardy, the entire world watched on the edge of their seats. Despite the tensions of the Cold War, the Soviet Union sent four ships to the landing area to help with the rescue. The Pope led a congregation of 10,000 in prayer for the astronauts' safe return, and 100,000 prayed in a festival in India. The US Senate passed a resolution urging businesses across the country to pause for a unified prayer. Seventy million Americans watched at least part of the telecast when the capsule finally returned to Earth.

From the time the crisis occurred on Apollo 13 until the eventual splashdown, four days elapsed. With Columbia, had NASA discovered the wing damage within a couple of days and sent the Atlantis for a rescue mission, they probably would have needed over a month to save the Columbia astronauts.

Would such a rescue have been expensive? Unbelievably. Tens of thousands of people would have had to gather to create the plans, make modifications to the Atlantis, and get it ready to fly. But no one would have batted an eye at the costs because the lives saved wouldn't just be statistical lives. One of the lives would have been Ilan Ramon's, a man born to Holocaust survivors, who helped defend his fledgeling young country in two wars, who blew up a nuclear reactor that could have empowered Saddam Hussein with a nuclear arsenal, potentially throwing the world into its first nuclear war. And that's just the story of one Columbia astronaut. The other six had stories of their own and loved ones to plead for their rescue. For a full month, the eyes of the world would have focused on the most extensive rescue mission of all time.

It could have been NASA's greatest moment.

Instead, it was a black mark against the space agency from which they literally never recovered. The Atlantis flight never flew. Two and a half years passed before a shuttle returned to space, and by then, the days of the shuttle program were numbered. The last launch occurred on July 8, 2011.

The ISS continued to function even without space shuttles transporting astronauts and supplies. Those functions were taken over by Russian Soyuz spacecraft. The United States, for so many decades the leader in space travel, took a backseat. The next time astronauts would blast off from US soil would be in 2020, but at that point, it wouldn't even be NASA taking them to space. The country wouldn't take back its edge in space exploration through its iconic space agency, but through private enterprise, with NASA contracting out to Elon Musk's SpaceX.

It's easy to blame NASA in hindsight for not taking greater steps to prevent the Columbia disaster. It's important to remember the analysis was anything but straightforward and none of us like to face the prospect of failure.

Early warning systems are a fabulous tool for pivoting quickly when failure looms ahead, but only when you're willing and able to adjust course based on their feedback. In the last chapter, we looked at how to build effective early warning systems. But it's not enough to get the warning if the early notice doesn't directly translate into changed action.

Here are a few pointers on how to make sure that your early warnings lead to effective action:

1. **Limit warnings to only true threats.** One of the biggest problem with early warning systems is that they can sometimes give off too many warnings. If your early warning system is too sensitive it might sound the alarm all the time for relatively minor issues. If that's the case, your team might already be trained to ignore the alarm when a true emergency comes.

2. **Assign responsibility.** Making sure it's clear to everyone who is responsible for responding to each type of warning.

3. **Limit Bureaucracy.** If there's an entire chain of command one needs to go through in order to act on the warning, the chances of an effective response plummet.

4. **Build emotional fortitude.** This is probably the hardest one on the list, but the truth is, sometimes when a warning goes off we'd rather not acknowledge it. The warning may indicate a failure, and in some organizations there might be a temptation to sweep the failure under the rug rather than bring it to light and deal with it. The more you can embrace failure, the easier it will be to take appropriate action when a warning is triggered.

Most of us have aspects of our lives or business we know aren't working, but we haven't wanted to face up to the problems and make the changes. We might have warning bells going off all around us, but we choose to ignore them. Take a moment and think about those areas where you're accepting less than the best. Write them down. Acknowledge them. And then ask yourself, if you weren't afraid of facing this area, what changes would you make?

CHAPTER 13

Quit like a Champion

"Failure isn't fatal, but failure to change might be."

- John Wooden

Dharma Butterfield was raised in the sleepy fishing village of Lund, British Columbia, growing up in a log cabin without running water or electricity. Dharma, like his parents before him, rebelled against the system he was raised in. His parents rebelled by fleeing the Vietnam draft, running to Canada, and raising their family in a commune. Dharma rebelled by changing his name to Stewart and teaching himself to code.

Stewart had a couple of modest successes early on, including Gradfinder.com, an early social network where users could locate and communicate with others in their graduating classes. He also created the unexpectedly popular 5K competition, where contestants attempted to build the best website under five kilobytes. But Stewart had a clear vision of what he wanted to create, and neither of these projects scratched his itch. His dream was to design a massively multiplayer online game, and his dream has since become a Silicon Valley legend.

Together with a couple of co-founders, including his then wife, Stewart founded Ludicorp and began building *Game Neverending*. But Game Never-Starting might have been a better name, for despite having a small cadre of informal users, it never reached its official launch.

Hurry Up and Fail

Clarity sometimes comes upon us in the darkest of situations. On a trip to New York, Stewart fell ill and spent a long night in his hotel barfing his guts out. By the time dawn came around, he'd had an inspiration.

While programming *Game Neverending*, Stewart and his partners created several elements to make the game function, including social chatting and object sharing. Stewart realized this functionality might have a different market, and if they could successfully spin off a successful side company, its income could fund further game development.

It took some convincing and a few backroom negotiations to get his partners on board with this new plan, but eventually, they accepted the idea of creating a "temporary" startup so they could get back to the core dream of building their video game. They named their app Flickr and built it for online photo sharing. Since the backbone of Flickr had already been built as part of *Game Neverending*, the team moved from development to launch in a mere three months.

Flickr was an instant hit. As with so many successful startups, growth was rapid and revenue couldn't keep pace. While paid plans were available, the constant need to upgrade infrastructure required all their money and more. However, when an internet startup generates serious traffic, funding is rarely hard to come by. The Ludicorp team faced a choice. Should they take on venture capital funding to keep the project going under their own auspices, or sell Flickr and resume their core mission?

In 2005, only a year after launching Flickr, the Ludicorp team sold it to Yahoo! for over $20 million. But even after the sale, Stewart and company couldn't get right back to business. Like so many startup exits, this one contained an earn-out provision that required the team to stay with Yahoo! for three or more years. In 2008, once his three-year commitment expired, Stewart sent in his now famous letter of resignation:

'In my 87 years service, I've accomplished many feats, shared in the ups and downs, made great friends and learned a tremendous amount...Those young baby boomers need their own try without us old 'uns standing in the way...So please accept my resignation, effective July 12. And I don't need no fancy parties or gold watches (I still have the one from '61 and '76). I will be spending more time with my family, tending to my small but growing alpaca herd and of course getting back to working with tin, my first love.'

Stewart was going back to working with his first love, but it wasn't tin. It was the dream of creating a massively multiplayer online game. The *Game Neverending* team were a group of unknown programmers, mostly working without wages to get their product off the ground. But their crazy side strategy actually worked, even if it did take them away from game development longer than they hoped. They had money in hand from the Flickr exit, but more importantly, they were now well-known in the venture capital world as the creators of one of the internet's hottest apps.

This time, money rolled in, and Stewart and Co. raised $17 million to start their next massively multiplayer online game, *Glitch*. Internet technology had come a long way since the days of *Game Neverending*. Not only were browsers better, but bandwidth was higher, allowing for a superior level of graphic interface. To play, players had to "learn how to find and grow resources, identify and build community and, at the higher levels of the game, proselytize to those around them."

But *Glitch* suffered from two fatal flaws. Firstly, the game was hard to explain. Stewart describes the world as *"Monty Python* meets Dr. Seuss." Gameplay included squeezing chickens to get eggs and milking butterflies (a vial of butterfly milk gave off the "tingly effervescence of a thousand tiny butterfly farts.") The difficulty of explaining the game slowed its spread, but there was an even bigger flaw: the game was programmed in Flash. Flash worked great on desktop computers, but not on mobile phones. When they started designing *Glitch*, smartphones were in their infancy. With each passing year, it became ever more clear that they could not just ignore the rapidly growing smartphone market.

While *Glitch* was steadily building a user-base, its incremental growth and lack of mobile presence signaled big challenges ahead. Silicon Valley VC firms have never subscribed to the "slow and steady wins the race" philosophy. *Glitch* was burning through cash, and Stewart could already foresee his second massively multiplayer online game ending in failure.

Despite having $5 million left in the bank, Stewart pulled the plug on Glitch. Massive layoffs were announced, and pretty soon only the four co-founders and four other staff members remained. But what would they do now? Most startups only collapse when they run out of money. Five million was still a substantial amount of dough, but what would they develop?

For the second time, Stewart and Co. realized that incidental to their video game creation, they had created something pretty cool with implications outside of gaming. With *Game Neverending*, the functionality that led to Flickr had been part of the game itself. This time, their discovery was a communications breakthrough their programmers had developed to coordinate their efforts.

Until this time, most internal company communications took place via email. Picture the following: a new hire joins a three-year-old startup. Day one, she's given her own corporate email address. She logs in and finds what? A standard welcome message from the CEO? Some notes on her health plan from HR? Most likely, she finds absolutely nothing.

She's joining a team that's had three years of collaboration before her arrival, much of that by email, and she has no access to their past conversations. Sure, one of her coworkers might go through his own inbox and forward her some of the more important messages, but the email system has severe limitations.

Emails systems are arranged for individuals, with everyone having a unique address. But the *Glitch* team built a more effective form of communication, divided by subject. Private conversations could still be held when necessary, but most *team* communications could be arranged topically. Each team member could join the topics relevant to their position and avoid the ones irrelevant. New staff members would have access to the entire history of a conversation, and the input of departing staff members wouldn't be deleted with their email accounts.

When the remaining *Glitch* team presented this software idea as a possible new direction for the company, their existing funders were hardly ecstatic. However, *Glitch* had already squandered the vast majority of its funding and their investors stood little chance of seeing *any* returns. So despite their lack of enthusiasm, they green-lighted the pivot from an online video game to an enterprise business software play.

These investors now look back at that decision as one of the wisest investments they've ever made. The new business communication tool, named Slack, became one of the fastest-growing apps in history, and on the day of its IPO in 2019, it opened at a $23 billion valuation.

Stewart Butterfield may now be the poster child for the startup pivot, but to me, he represents something much greater: The ability to see value hidden in plain sight. If his games were more successful, he might never have built his iconic companies. Until *Glitch* failed, their team had only developed Slack for their own internal use, oblivious they were sitting on a goldmine of innovative technology.

Quitters get a bad rap. I once had a friend brag he'd spent fourteen years in a job he hated. "You have to give me credit, I stuck it out and didn't quit until I was absolutely sure I couldn't make it work." I was stunned. I could understand if he had a family to feed and no other source of income. Then perhaps I'd admire his resolve to keep pushing despite his misery. But the guy had no such financial pressure. He just didn't want to be a "quitter."

While quitters get mocked, the Stewart Butterfields of the world are praised for identifying what's not working and pivoting to something better. And before you object, saying quitting and pivoting are two different things, remember Stewart pulled the plug on *Glitch* with no contingency plan *before* he and his team came up with the idea for Slack.

In my personal experience, as long as I'm following a failing path, I rarely have the mental bandwidth to pivot. While it's possible Butterfield could've thought of Slack while working on *Glitch*, having a blank slate gave his team room to think and be creative.

Is it time for you to put on the breaks and maybe consider a new path? How can you tell if you just need to hunker down and push through your challenges or if it really is time to blow up your old strategy and pivot to a new one? There's no clear-cut formula that can answer the question, but considering the following factors can help you gain clarity:

1. **Key performance indicators (KPI's).** KPI's are specific and quantifiable measurements that help businesses track progress towards strategic goals. Common business examples include sales revenue, conversion rate, lifetime customer value, and customer acquisition cost, but you can have KPI's in non-business settings as well. If your KPI's are consistently below expectations or targets, despite your attempts to improve them, it might be time to pivot.

2. **Market response.** How quickly are you gaining traction in the marketplace? If your customer feedback is phenomenal and your sales traction slow, you might just need to pivot your marketing strategy. But if sales are slow and feedback only lukewarm, it might be time to pivot entirely.

3. **Changes in the market.** Are there any changes in the market like new competition, technology advancements or regulatory changes? Stewart Butterfield saw the technological advancement of smart phones and realized that a game programmed in Flash would become more and more obsolete if he didn't pivot.

4. **Financial health.** Are you burning through cash with no remedy in sight? You might want to pivot before your resources run out.

5. **Team morale.** If your team is frustrated, unmotivated, or burnt out, it could be an indication that your current path isn't working.

6. **Innovation and opportunity.** If there's a new opportunity or innovation that aligns with your business's strengths and could offer better growth prospects, it might be worth pivoting.

Once you make the decision to pivot, here are a few steps to help make your new direction more successful than your last.

1. **Strategic planning.** Clearly define your new direction, goals, and strategies. This might involve a new business model, new target market, new product or service, or new marketing strategy.

2. **Market research.** Understand your new market, including customer needs, competitor landscape, and potential challenges. This will help you refine your strategies and offerings.

3. **Get all stakeholders on board.** You want everyone involved, including staff, investors, customers, and partners, to embrace the change in direction. Explain why the pivot is necessary and how it will benefit them. Note that you might not retain everyone, and that parting ways with those who can not embrace the new direction might be a necessary cost of pivoting.

4. **Make sure you have sufficient resources.** Do you have sufficient financial, human, and technical resources to successfully pivot?

5. **Monitoring and adjustments.** Just because you pivoted once doesn't mean you won't need to do so again. Continue to monitor your KPI's and be open to making further adjustments if necessary.

A successful pivot requires commitment, flexibility, and resilience. It's a challenging process, but with careful planning and execution, it can breathe new life into a struggling project.

How good are you at mitigating failure?
Find out with our Failure Scorecard at
DaveMasonAuthor.com/failure-scorecard

PART 5

Don't Fail on Others

CHAPTER 14

Own Your Failures

"Failure doesn't define you. It's what you do after you fail that determines whether you are a leader or a waste of perfectly good air."

—SABAA TAHIR

When my wife and I launched the online course mentioned at the beginning of this book, we told attendees we had no idea what we were doing, and we fully intended to mess up quite a few things. Live on Zoom, we witnessed students' reactions to this bizarre opening statement. What did they do? They laughed and then cheered.

But why?

Imagine getting on a plane and the pilot says, "This is my first time actually flying one of these, and I expect I'll make plenty of mistakes, but don't worry, I've spent over 100 hours in a flight simulator, and I've watched *Airplane* half a dozen times, so I feel pretty confident I can fix any trouble that arises."

Would you laugh? Probably. But only because you wouldn't take the pilot seriously. If you did, you might pull open the emergency door and jump down to the tarmac.

Imagine going into surgery and learning just as they start the anesthesia that your surgeon has never operated before. Or going into court and learning your attorney has never defended anyone before. Would you be laughing under such circumstances?

So why did course participants cheer when we told them we'd never taught this before?

There are three factors, which we'll cover in the next three chapters.

Hurry Up and Fail

The first is that we took the risk upon ourselves.

The reason you wouldn't feel comfortable boarding a plane with an inexperienced pilot, being operated on by an inexperienced surgeon, or being represented by an inexperienced attorney is if they mess up, you bear the consequences.

Essential to the philosophy of *Hurry up and Fail* is that no one else should have to suffer for your mistakes. We call this Risk Reversal.

I get called all the time by salespeople who are supremely confident their product or service will benefit my business. They paint a picture of all the additional sales I'll make, of all the additional profit I'll enjoy. I always ask them the same question, "Can you guarantee your results?" 99% of the time, they won't.

I call this sales approach "Pay and Pray." They want me to pay upfront for their product or service and then pray it actually yields the promised results. This makes no sense to me. If they're so confident of their results, why am I the one bearing the risk?

The participants in *Dream, Design, Manifest* weren't at all stressed because we had eliminated their downside. When they signed up, we gave them all what we called our 10X guarantee. We committed to offering them value equivalent to 10 times what they paid for the course. If they paid $100 for the course and at the end felt they only received $900 worth of value, they could get a full refund and enjoy the entire course for free. I did the same with my Financial Fundamentals course, guaranteeing participants would raise their net worth by at least 10 times the amount they paid for the course. If they didn't, they could get a full refund, and the course would remain theirs to enjoy for free.

It shocks me more businesses don't employ Risk Reversal, because it's such a powerful force. Imagine the following scenario: a business owner wants to redesign the graphics on an underperforming ad campaign and gets quotes from two contractors, Stan and Jane. Stan quotes a price of $500, proudly claims he won't be undersold, and is confident everyone will be thrilled with his work. But when you ask about a guarantee, he says, "I can't do that. I need to be compensated for my time, right? But don't worry, I know I'll do a great job."

Jane's pitch is totally different. "I have a concept I think will work great for you," she says, "but the truth is, no one ever knows 100% how the public will respond to an ad. So here's my offer: I'll charge $1000 for the ad redesign. I'm not the cheapest option out there, but I stand by my work. In fact, I'll guarantee you'll see at least $2000 in new revenue from my ad during the first month it runs, otherwise I'll refund the full $1000 payment, and you can keep the ad as my gift."

Which of those contractors would you select?

If it was me, it wouldn't even be close. I'd gladly pay more for someone who stands by her work.

Just by adding this Risk Reversing provision, Jane can charge twice as much for her time and close a higher percentage of deals. Even if she winds up missing her target 25% of the time, she'll still come out way ahead.

With *Dream, Design, Manifest*, we had over fifty paid attendees, and exactly two of them asked for their money back. One watched a single session and decided our course wasn't for her. Another thought she'd have time for the course but didn't, and she might still come back and take it in the future. But by offering the guarantee, we probably signed up an additional 15 participants who were on the fence and wouldn't have committed otherwise.

There's a cockiness, an arrogance, that people commonly associate with salespeople. We assume they're not seeking our benefit but their own. The more doubts we voice, the more assurances they offer. Of course, as I pointed out earlier, these assurances normally stop short of a guarantee.

My advice? Drop the assurances and stand behind results. My wife Chana has used this tactic successfully in her coaching business. Potential clients fear they'll wind up in a "black hole." Many tell stories of seeing the same therapist for years and spending tens of thousands of dollars, only to make zero progress.

Chana, on the other hand, is all about results. She'll only work with clients she believes she'll help and calms their fears with Risk Reversal, a technique almost unheard of among therapists.

I do the same thing in my Strategic Business Coaching practice. If someone is paying me thousands of dollars for business advice, I want them to be making at least ten times as much from working with me. If I don't think they have the potential to hit those numbers, I won't take them on as a client. And if I do take them on, I'll back up my work with a full money back guarantee.

Many coaches try to accomplish the same thing in a less effective manner by offering free trial sessions. I don't advocate giving away your time for free. Offering valuable services for nothing devalues them, implying you don't value your time. Standing behind results does the exact opposite. It shows you're confident, and believe you're worth every penny.

Risk Reversal can be your psychological safety net. Many of us fear promoting ourselves because we question our ability to deliver the goods. We don't want to take someone's money and come up short. Rather than holding yourself back, move forward in a way that ensures only you will bear the consequences of your failures. Let's look at a few elements that can help you construct strong risk reversal:

1. **What are the biggest fears you need to address?** Consider polling potential clients and customers to find out what their fears are. Once you know them, you can start to address them.

2. **How can you remove or reduce that fear?** Would a free trial eliminate that fear? A satisfaction guarantee? A results guarantee? What would make your offer irresistible?

3. **How can you minimize the downside to yourself?** In Chana's coaching business, she allows clients to get a full refund on a 12 session coaching package if they're not satisfied after the first session. This way, she only risks losing an hour of her time, not all 12 hours.

Risk Reversal can ease concerns that working with you will be a costly mistake. As mentioned above, it's a great tool for your sales process, allowing you to close more clients and potentially charge a premium. But Risk Reversal alone does little to enhance a client's experience of working with you. In the next two chapters, we'll examine two other factors that can cause others to forgive or even celebrate your failures.

CHAPTER 15

Exceed Expectations

"If you're not prepared to be wrong, you'll never come up with anything original."

- KEN ROBINSON

Marie Forleo is among the most impactful teachers of small business tactics in the world, with her weekly videos periodically topping a million views and her premier program, B-School, drawing over 10,000 new students a year.

The first time I checked out B-School, the program looked great, but I couldn't bring myself to pull the trigger. Why not? First was the $2000 price tag, steep for an online course. Second, I feared the material would be too introductory. But the third reason was the true deal breaker. I didn't know if I was eligible, and I was too embarrassed to ask.

B-School teaches a concept known as the Ideal Customer Avatar (ICA). Rather than targeting your marketing to everyone, Marie encourages you to choose a single individual who represents your ideal customer and target your marketing for them. When I first looked at B-School's marketing, it was easy to reverse engineer Marie's ICA. Everything from color schemes and font selections to the interviews she published with B-School alumni showed she was targeting her course to women in their thirties looking to transition from employees to entrepreneurs. While nothing stated the course was only for women, the complete lack of men made me wonder if I was even welcome.

I didn't join until the following year, when I heard an interview between Marie and Jairek Robbins, where he pointed out that before taking the course his first time, he'd wondered if men were allowed in (Marie has since added a

Hurry Up and Fail

few men to her marketing materials to remove this doubt). Much as I enjoyed B-School, I got more value from observing how Marie constructed and ran the course to deliver maximum value.

One technique that left a deep impression was Marie's reliance on secret bonuses, components she hadn't breathed a word about during promotion that were thrown in as extras during the course. My favorite bonus was a behind-the-scenes look at the mechanisms that powered B-School, which taught me about course construction and how to manage a large community.

At first, the idea of including secret bonuses struck me as counterintuitive. Remember, Marie was billing $2000 for an online course. To get participants to pay that much, wouldn't she want to *boast* about every bit of value? Why offer benefits you intentionally leave out of your advertising?

The answer is that Marie wasn't just thinking of the initial sale alone. The last thing she wanted was for people to sign up, believe they didn't get their money's worth, and say that her course was a ripoff. Rather, Marie wanted past students to become her biggest advocates. And one way to turn customers into advocates is to Over Deliver.

Over Delivering is the second of the three factors that minimize the impact of failures. It goes hand in hand with Risk Reversal, as the more you Over Deliver, the less likely customers are to ask for refunds.

One note of caution on Over Delivery, it works best when it comes as a surprise. Had Marie included her bonuses in her promotional materials, they'd no longer be viewed as extras but expectations. When you give surprise bonuses, you delight customers in ways you never could by simply fulfilling promises.

Ideally, you want everyone who works with you to feel like you've Over Delivered. As we'll see in the next example, Over Delivery has little connection to the actual value your customers receive. It's a relative measure based solely on expectations.

Let's contrast my B-School experience with an incident that occurred a few hours before I wrote the first draft of this section.

At the time, my newest obsession was AppSumo, a software site that offers absolutely insane deals. For instance, I bought a graphic editor that normally costs $96 a year, but on AppSumo I got lifetime (not yearly) access for only $49. At first, I couldn't figure out how they could offer deals so inexpensively. Then I realized their secret sauce. Because they have such a strong, active community, any company they feature gets massive exposure. The top apps in each niche would never undermine their own pricing by giving away such deals, but newer brands looking to make a name for themselves can scale up quickly by working with AppSumo.

Reviews are key on AppSumo, and I've found them extremely reliable. Smart brands engage with the Sumolings (the community members) to generate strong buzz for their product. Still, I was unprepared for what happened the second time I bought a lifetime license, this time for a social media scheduling app.

Within a few days, I received an email from the CEO offering to personally give me a demonstration of the platform. While I knew companies worked hard to impress the Sumolings, I wasn't expecting that level of service. I clicked to book a time on the CEO's personal calendar. Since the company was willing to go to such efforts, I anticipated a valuable call and paid one of my staff to also attend so she could familiarize herself with the platform.

We both logged on early and eager to learn. A woman from the company joined us, quickly stated her name, and launched into her training, which felt so rote, it was either memorized or read off her monitor. I finally managed to interrupt her and ask, "Where's the CEO?"

"Oh, he's too busy to do these calls himself."

So the CEO had no intention of conducting the demonstration, which left me both frustrated and scratching my head. Why make such an offer if you don't aim to deliver? We all know salespeople often overpromise to make a sale, but in this case, I'd already bought their product, and I owned a lifetime subscription, so they clearly weren't doing it to get more of my money. I expect they were hoping to cultivate goodwill. And offering a free demonstration could be an excellent avenue for goodwill. But in this case, because they promised the CEO himself, it set an awfully high bar. When they failed to live up to that bar, it created a negative impression, not a positive one. In the end, I left them a review entitled, "Overpromised, Under Delivered."

This was the exact opposite of B-School, which under-promised and Over Delivered. That much should be obvious. But I want to focus your attention on an aspect of the dynamic that may not be so clear. Absolute value played no role.

B-School is a $2000 program. That's a serious amount of money to pay for an online course. Yet, because Marie threw in a few unexpected bonus trainings, I walked away feeling I got more than I bargained for, and I've circulated positive reviews ever since.

With the social media app, I got an absolute steal on the software. The value for my money was through the roof. Then the company offered a free one-on-one training, which they didn't have to do and which I wasn't expecting; it should have left an extremely positive impression. But because they made a claim they didn't stand by, I was left with a bad taste in my mouth and docked the company one taco as a result (yes, Sumolings give reviews in tacos, not stars).

By any objective standard, I got a greater bang for my buck with the app than with B-School. But human emotions aren't logical and calculating. I felt honored to receive the B-School bonuses but manipulated and fooled by the software company.

When it comes to Hurrying up and Failing, your audience will be incredibly forgiving as long as you deliver what you promise, and they'll be thrilled if you deliver more. When we created *Dream, Design, Manifest*, we promised participants six two-hour sessions. But since we weren't experts in teaching the material online and didn't know where our students would struggle, we kept looking for opportunities to add more value. Each week we offered bonus sessions, many of them created on the spot to address weaknesses we identified in our own curriculum or additional needs of our audience. For instance, a number of our students were looking to start their own businesses, so I threw in a bonus class on my favorite business principles.

Next time we run the course, I expect our core curriculum will be stronger, and as a result, we might choose to add fewer bonus sessions. But we'll always try to offer value we haven't advertised as part of the course.

Before leaving this section, take a moment to think about your own offerings. Are there elements you can add to your offering that will surprise and delight your clients? Here are a few tips to help you exceed expectations:

1. **Brainstorm a range of low-cost, high-value bonus offerings.** What are additional things you can give your clients, above and beyond your core product or service that they will love? To avoid killing your profit margins, try to create bonuses that give your clients strong value, but cost you little to deliver. For instance, if you're selling a paperback book, your clients might be delighted to get a second paperback for free, but your cost to print and deliver a second book can add up. A video course that goes deeper into the lessons of the book might be more effective because once it's created you can give access to thousands of clients for minimal additional cost.

2. **Divide your bonuses into those you include in your initial offer and those you'll reveal later.** Potential clients need to be sold on the value they'll get from your product or service. One of the most effective ways of raising the perceived value is by offering bonuses as part of the sign up. Select a few of the bonuses you've created and include them with your offer. Just know that the bonuses you added into your initial offer will not make clients feel you're going above and beyond for them. Once

they're part of the offer, they've now become expectations. That's why you want to hold some bonuses back for later.

3. **Keep your secret bonuses secret.** It's so hard to hold back from telling potential customers all they're going to get. Especially when you have someone sitting on the fence, you just want to spill the beans and tell them there's so much more than they know. Restrain yourself. Even hinting that you'll be giving secret bonuses later on can kill the impact these bonuses will eventually have.

4. **Gather feedback along the way.** You may think you've put together a fabulous offering, but once your clients start engaging with it, they might find it lacking in ways you didn't expect. That knowledge can be gold. If your client feedback shows you holes in your offering, rush in to fill them. Creating additional bonuses to fix the problems in your initial offer may leave clients more impressed than if you'd created a flawless product to begin with.

5. **Use Limited-Time Risk Reversal.** Allow your customers a window of time where they can get their money back if unsatisfied. So if you have a six-week course, you may offer a money-back guarantee during the first two weeks. Make sure to launch some of your secret bonuses during this period to really blow everyone away. But just offering the guarantee can increase satisfaction with your product.

6. **Follow-up.** Everyone wants to be heard. Even a client with a lukewarm experience will feel better if they have a chance to make their voice heard. Be open to honest feedback, and make sure you actually take time to read it and respond appropriately.

The first two elements we've looked at in this chapter can make people more forgiving of your failures. Risk reversal can ensure your clients won't suffer financial loss if dissatisfied. And if you can make your products go beyond expectations in one area, your clients will be more likely to overlook other areas where you may have fallen short. But wouldn't it be great if you could find a way for your clients to not only put up with your failures, but actively enjoy going through the learning process with you? This final section will show you a way to accomplish exactly that. Just be forewarned, you may not like it.

CHAPTER 16

Nurture Belonging

"There is no innovation and creativity without failure. Period."

- BRENÉ BROWN

Which of the following would you pay more for?

1. A Beta edition of a raw, unfinished product; or

2. That same product once all the kinks have been worked out

The obvious answer is the latter. Indeed, the heavy discounts on AppSumo are the main reason Sumolings are willing to buy an app that might still lag behind the market leaders. But wouldn't it be nice if you could figure out a way to charge a premium for your unfinished product?

Let's go back to our old friend Russell Brunson and look at the release of his most recent book, *Traffic Secrets*. Though it contains his secrets for increasing website traffic, the book itself was anything but a secret. For more than a year before its release, Russell hinted, teased, and plugged it every chance he got. Russell's built an incredibly active community around himself and his company, ClickFunnels, and his plugs created tons of anticipation.

But even as he was building anticipation, he still needed to produce an amazing book. Russell will be the first to tell you writing isn't his forte. He shines on stage. Whereas I write draft after draft of my books to improve my material, Russell likes to hone his material by teaching it live.

Hurry Up and Fail

I have a digital copy of the finished, final edition of *Traffic Secrets*, for which I paid $0.99 on Amazon. So if the final product, with Russel's thoughts fully organized, is only worth a buck, what do you think it would be worth to watch him deliver the raw, unorganized lessons? A dime perhaps? A quarter at most?

Hardly. Only Russell's elite inner circle were privileged to hear him teach the early versions live, and they paid thousands of dollars each for the chance.

Obviously, the comparison between an ebook and an in-person event is a silly one. But don't let that distract you from the key point. We expect discounts for Beta-editions, but will gladly pay more for early access to exclusive content. We'll pay less for unpolished content but more to participate in the launch of something new even if it doesn't have all the bugs worked out.

Is the difference just spin?

Samsung makes excellent phones, but no one camps out to get the first crack at a new Samsung. So why will they do so for a new iPhone? It's not because anyone in line has a pressing need to make a phone call. Or send a text. Or take a photo. Or listen to a song. Virtually everyone waiting for hours outside the Apple store already has a device with nearly identical functionality. Sure, their current phone might have a few cracks in the screen or be running a tad slow, but is their need for a new phone so dire they couldn't have waited a couple of days to buy it without the line?

Of course not. No one lines up for the new iPhone because of a technological need. They're there for the same reason I stood in long lines as a kid to see *The Empire Strikes Back* and *Return of the Jedi* on the day they were released. I wanted the excitement of being among the *first* to see the new *Star Wars* movies, before I heard about them from anyone else. I wanted to be one of the kids at school talking about the movie rather than plugging my ears to avoid spoilers. And did I mind standing in line for movie tickets? Absolutely not. I was there amongst my tribe.

There are incoming freshman at Duke University who look forward to camping out for weeks to get basketball tickets. As much as they enjoy basketball, if you handed them free tickets and told them they didn't need to wait, many would be disappointed. Camping out for tickets has become part of the culture of the university. For the rest of their lives, Duke alumni tell the stories of how they camped out with other fanatic fans to get the best tickets. The experience itself is part of their identity.

The best brands make customers feel like they're a *part of something*. The people who pay Russell Brunson thousands of dollars to hear him stumble through his early, raw presentations on *Traffic Secrets* weren't only there to be with Russel or to learn new marketing tactics. They show up for each other as well. They're there because Brunson's succeeded in one of the hardest and most powerful areas of brand building. He's created a community. And not just a community, a culture. In fact, Russel calls it a "Cult-ure" because of the fanatical, cult-like energy of his followers. ClickFunnels groupies literally go on cruises together. Cruises! Around digital marketing of all things.

This third way of minimizing the downside of your failures is by far the hardest to execute. Anyone can offer a money-back guarantee. Anyone can offer surprise bonuses. Both of those categories focus on your offerings. This third area is all about *you*.

Simply put, those who identify with you and want you to succeed will be far more forgiving of your failures. They'll be excited about your journey and want to come along for the ride, even when there are bumps in the road.

Think about any brand or movement you've ever fallen in love with. Chances are, it wasn't just because of a great product, but because of a powerful vision you desired to connect with. And most likely an individual who represented that vision.

Again, Samsung makes a great phone. But I haven't the slightest idea who built the company or what distinguishes them. Apple's cult-like following didn't just happen. Steve Jobs built it. His ads didn't focus on processing speed, but to "Think Different." Steve told us the power of individual expression we'd unlock with a Mac would stop the year 1984 from being like the book *1984*.

How many car commercials have you seen touting horsepower, bucket seats, cup holders and the like? My son is obsessed with Tesla, and I assure you he couldn't care less about the cup holders. He loves the company because Elon Musk has a vision that goes beyond selling cars. Musk speaks about global challenges and how to build a sustainable future through technology. Tesla has suffered through one high-profile mistake after another, but fans shrug them off. It doesn't even matter if Nissan releases a new version of the all electric Leaf that's cheaper than the comparable Tesla. When you're a fan, you're not price shopping because your buying choices are part of your *identity*.

So how does one build a base of raving fans so excited to journey with you they'll forgive mistakes along the way? Let's briefly look at three aspects: person, message, and community.

Hurry Up and Fail

1. **Person**

When presenting ourselves to others, especially to would-be clients, we have an innate desire to cover up our flaws, to make ourselves sound better than we are. Here's a warning: if you present yourself as infallible, don't expect others to forgive your blunders.

Contrary to popular belief, you don't have to be incredibly charismatic to get people to care about you and your mission. If you are real, present, and vulnerable with your audience, they'll be real, present, and forgiving in return. The more you open up to your audience, the more they'll open up to you.

2. **Mission**

What is it your business stands for? If it's simply that you offer a good product at a good price, then don't be surprised if your customers jump ship when a competitor offers a better product or price. But if you have a true mission you share with your audience, those who believe in the mission won't go running to a competitor with slightly higher specs or a slightly lower price tag.

3. **Community**

Founders can be tyrants when it comes to their brand, product, or project. The need to maintain control is so common its even got its own name: founder's syndrome. But to build fierce loyalty, it's important to create the space for others to step up. At a certain point during *Dream, Design, Manifest*, a couple of participants started a Mastermind group, and they recruited other students in the class to join them. Part of me wanted to protest and say, "Hey, this is our show. What are you doing stepping up and taking the lead?" Fortunately, the wiser part bit my tongue and let it happen. No one was stepping on our toes. Rather, they were saying the work we'd done together was important enough that they wanted to continue integrating it together even after the class came to an end.

Those Duke freshmen who camp out for weeks aren't just there for basketball tickets, they're there to be with each other. Standing in line for the new iPhone with other Apple fans or waiting for *Return of the Jedi* tickets with other *Star Wars* fans adds to the excitement of the event. When your brand reaches beyond you, beyond your products or services, and others find a community of peers under your banner, when it becomes part of their identity, they'll graciously tolerate a few bumps in the road.

Who pays the price for your failures?
Take our Failure Scorecard at
DaveMasonAuthor.com/failure-scorecard

Epilogue

I needed a miracle.

And I had an idea where to find one.

I live in Jerusalem, just a half hour walk from the Western Wall. There's an obscure legend that if one goes to the Wall for 40 consecutive days and prays for a single thing, they'll be answered. I had no idea where this legend came from--it's certainly not recorded in any of Judaism's foundational texts--but I was desperate and had little to lose.

My desperation came from a string of costly business decisions that put me in real danger of losing not only my company, but my house as well. Without seeing an easy way out, I committed to put in my 40 days.

Each evening, I walked to the Western Wall and prayed for a miraculous turnaround. True to the promise, within 40 days, I received my answer. But as an attorney, I should have been smart enough to read the fine print. The legend promised me an answer, but not necessarily the one I wanted.

Halfway through my 40 days, I stood with my forehead against the wall when a flash of clarity boomed in my head. It said, "Stop being such an idiot! Don't expect some miraculous influx of cash to return your business to profitability. Stop avoiding the hard decisions and get to work!"

That slap in the face was exactly what I needed to wake up and see the obvious. My business strategy until then had been the very antithesis of what I teach in this book.

I'd enjoyed early business success, largely based on being in the right place at the right time, which fooled me into thinking I knew more about business than I actually did. I made decisions more from my gut than from solid business principles. I rarely gathered feedback on what was actually working and what wasn't. When something failed, I didn't conduct post-mortems to learn from the experience. Nor did I do pre-mortems when starting new projects to identify potential pitfalls.

Probably the most damaging mistake was a close corollary to the fear of rejection: my fear of rejecting others. I struggled to set clear expectations for staff, and I hated firing people. The result was a bloated company with a higher payroll than our revenue could support.

The cuts I made in the weeks following my Western Wall epiphany were some of the most painful I've made in over two decades in business. I fired more than half my staff, closed my offices, and slashed underperforming segments of my business. I also started becoming a student of business. I had to face the fact that I had no clue what I was doing.

You'll often hear personal growth gurus say, "the way you do one thing is the way you do everything." This doesn't match my experience at all. If this were true, we wouldn't see Hall of Fame athletes filing for bankruptcy. We wouldn't see Oscar winning actors on their fourth marriages. In my case, there were areas in my business where I excelled and others where I flailed. Not surprisingly, I thrived in areas where I was willing to fall on my face repeatedly, and I struggled in areas I avoided.

Whenever I pivot from being too scared to act to embracing a Hurry up and Fail mindset, I prime myself for a huge wave of growth. That's what I experienced when I shifted from avoiding the camera to publishing daily videos. I felt it again when I stopped ignoring bad stock picks and started dancing to my Failure playlist. And it's what's fueled my business turnaround once I stopped burying my head in the sand and made the hard choices.

Are there are areas in life you prefer to avoid? Flipping the switch from avoidance to Hurrying up and Failing can be just the thing you need to experience massive growth.

I wish you the very best on your Hurry Up and Fail journey. You can share your experiences with me and the rest of the community by using the tag #HurryUpandFail.

Acknowledgments

This book has been a fabulous opportunity to share lessons that I've derived from some of the greatest teachers and role models I've had. The pages are packed with examples taken from courses I've taken from educators including Russell Brunson, Marie Forleo, Sara Blakely and so many more who I won't list here as their names are sprinkled throughout the book.

Behind the scenes, I'm eternally grateful to my wife Chana and my son Aryeh Lev, who humor my book projects and put many hours into reading and editing my work.

Victor Da Silva was invaluable in the early goings as a researcher to help me locate amazing examples to illustrate the points I wanted to make in the book.

A special thanks to all members of *Dream, Design, Manifest*, the group that showed so much enthusiasm in response to my impromptu use of the term, Hurry Up and Fail. It was that reaction that make me think I'd stumbled upon something special and motivated me to create this book.

Notes

Chapter 1: Embrace Failure

The Sara Blakely story told here was pieced together from several sources, including Sara's class on Entrepreneurship on Masterclass.com, her interview with Tony Robbins, available at https://www.youtube.com/watch?v=9JrAojUqMvQ, and her interview with Guy Raz on NPR's How I Built This Podcast, available at https://www.npr.org/transcripts/493312213?storyId=493312213?storyId=493312213

The Forbes article discussing Sara becoming a billionaire can be found at https://www.forbes.com/sites/clareoconnor/2012/03/07/undercover-billionaire-sara-blakely-joins-the-rich-list-thanks-to-spanx/?sh=523d7810d736

Ralph Waldo Emerson actually said, "If a man has good corn or wood, or boards, or pigs, to sell, or can make better chairs or knives, crucibles or church organs, than anybody else, you will find a broad hard-beaten road to his house, though it be in the woods."

https://en.wikipedia.org/wiki/Build_a_better_mousetrap,_and_the_world_will_beat_a_path_to_your_door

The Wikipedia article on NLP can be found at https://en.wikipedia.org/wiki/Neuro-linguistic_programming

Chapter 2: Lower the Stakes

Much of the description of the Everest climb comes from Jon Krakauer's book, Into Thin Air.

For the story of Beck Weathers, see https://en.wikipedia.org/wiki/Beck_Weathers.

Chapter 3: Start Before You're Ready

The stories of Frank Abagnale mainly come from his autobiography, Catch Me If You Can, and there are additional references to the movie by the same name.

An estimated 70% of people will suffer from imposter syndrome at some point in their lives. [Sakulku, J. (1). The Impostor Phenomenon. The Journal of Behavioral Science, 6(1), 75-97. https://doi.org/10.14456/ijbs.2011.6]

Jack Kerouac writing On The Road, https://en.wikipedia.org/wiki/On_the_Road

The story of Chris Baty and NaNoWriMo largely comes from his book, <u>No Plot? No Problem! A Low-Stress, High-Velocity Guide to Writing a Novel in 30 Days</u>, as well as an interview I conducted with Chris. Other sources include https://www.wikiwrimo.org/wiki/National_Novel_Writing_Month and http://www.mebondbooks.com/2016/11/14/history-nanowrimo/

Chapter 4: Fail Fast, Fail Cheap

For details on the story on Nick Swinmurn and Zappos, see https://www.businessinsider.com/nick-swinmurn-zappos-rnkd-2011-11, and https://en.wikipedia.org/wiki/Tony_Hsieh, and listen to the How I Built This episode at https://www.npr.org/2019/05/15/723670593/zappos-tony-hsieh.

For the Mechanical Turk story, see https://www.britannica.com/story/the-mechanical-turk-ai-marvel-or-parlor-trick, and The Chess World: A Magazine: Volume VIII, page 3.

For information on Amazon's MTurk, see: https://www.mturk.com/worker#:~:text=These%20include%20tasks%20such%20as,available%20on%20Amazon%20Mechanical%20Turk%3F

Aaron Koblin's MTurk sheep project can be found at http://www.thesheepmarket.com/ but unfortunately can no longer be viewed on most browsers as it was created in Flash.

To learn more about the segment on business cards and Card Much see https://www.economist.com/business/2015/03/12/on-the-cards and https://thenextweb.com/insider/2014/05/07/linkedin-shuts-cardmunch-business-card-converter-app-offers-evernote-alternative/

For the Wizard of Oz paradigm, see https://en.wikipedia.org/wiki/Wizard_of_Oz_experiment

For the One Painkiller technique, see https://www.robotmascot.co.uk/18-types-of-minimum-viable-product/

Learn more about Joe Gebbia and AirBNB at https://www.npr.org/2017/10/19/543035808/airbnb-joe-gebbia

Read about the Fung Wah bus at https://www.yelp.com/biz/fung-wah-bus-boston?sort_by=rating_asc and https://www.theguardian.com/us-news/2015/jul/17/fung-wah-new-york-city-worst-bus-company

For more on Dropbox and Drew Houston, see https://www.npr.org/2020/11/06/932199300/dropbox-drew-houston

For more on the Cybertruck, see https://www.fool.com/investing/2019/12/02/tesla-cybertruck-orders-are-pouring-in-but-investo.aspx

Chapter 5: Learn to Love Rejection

Steven King discusses his Happy Stamps story in his autobiographical book <u>On Writing</u>.

Details about S&H Green Stamps were taken from https://www.youtube.com/watch?v=0qciBdzaajw and https://www.mcall.com/news/mc-xpm-1984-10-16-2449082-story.html

Learn about the gender pay gap at https://www.payscale.com/data/gender-pay-gap.

For Jia Jang's story, see his book Rejection Proof and his TED Talk at https://www.ted.com/talks/jia_jiang_what_i_learned_from_100_days_of_rejection

For more on Rejection Therapy, see https://www.npr.org/sections/health-shots/2015/01/16/377239011/by-making-a-game-out-of-rejection-a-man-conquers-fear

Notes

Chapter 6: Fail Small, Fail Often

For Jordan Harbinger's discussion of his social anxiety, see his talk at Google at https://www.youtube.com/watch?v=buUw3rGcEic

The course I took with Russel Brunson and Stephen Larson was called One Funnel Away. The course used to be offered frequently and could be found at https://www.onefunnelaway.com/challenge?cf_affiliate_id=704697&affiliate_id=704697, but it has since been replaced with a shorter course called My First Funnel Challenge which can be found at https://www.yourfirstfunnelchallenge.com/yffc?aff=4da58c85-317d-4bcc-9b45-661f12c25e0f-1WzEwLDExMDBd0.

For Forbes discussing Jordan Harbinger's relationship building, see https://www.forbes.com/sites/jrose/2018/05/31/how-to-connect-with-anyone/?sh=3a9c9f5a77a9

Jordan Harbinger's Six Minute Networking course can be found at https://www.jordanharbinger.com/courses/

Tom Bilyeu's discussion of Jordan Harbinger can be found at https://www.youtube.com/watch?v=Rx-TNupNU8Q

My interview on Doc Green's Earn and Invest podcast can be found at https://diversefi.com/2020/05/04/episode-103the-most-important-financial-book-you-havent-discovered-yet/

Chapter 7: Seek Feedback

The line about science fiction that follows the laws of relativity being relatively boring was read years ago in a Monty (formerly Robot Man) comic strip by Jim Meddick. I remember the line, but could not track down the specific strip that used it.

All quotes from Mark Watney are from the book The Martian. The movie is not quoted at all.

For Pixar's results on Toy Story, see https://en.wikipedia.org/wiki/Toy_Story

Michael Eisner's quote about Pixar can be found in the Steve Jobs biography by Walter Isaacson, as can the Steve Jobs quote discussing Eisner.

For Finding Nemo results, see https://en.wikipedia.org/wiki/Finding_Nemo

Most of the quotes on the Pixar creative process come from Catmull's book Creativity Inc.

Catmull's quote about the Braintrust being where movies going from sucking to not sucking comes from the book The Culture Code by Daniel Coyle.

Chapter 8: Investigate Failure

For the history of the Black Box, see https://www.wired.com/2010/03/0317warren-invents-airplane-black-box/

Ethiopian air crash https://www.businessinsider.com/ethiopian-airlines-et302-boeing-737-max-crash-timeline-2019-4#there-were-few-pieces-of-wreckage-left-that-were-large-enough-for-you-to-be-able-to-tell-it-was-a-plane-12

Plane crash statistics, http://planecrashinfo.com/cause.htm

Sidney Dekker, https://www.humanfactors.lth.se/fileadmin/lusa/Sidney_Dekker/books/DekkersFieldGuide.pdf

For Southwest's financials, see http://investors.southwest.com/~/media/Files/S/Southwest-IR/2012_SouthwestAirlinesOneReport.pdf

The impact of the new Airbus model. https://www.theverge.com/2019/5/2/18518176/boeing-737-max-crash-problems-human-error-mcas-faa

The rebate to Southwest if they needed to retrain pilots: https://www.reuters.com/article/us-boeing-airplane-southwest/u-s-lawmakers-question-boeings-1-mln-rebate-clause-for-southwest-737-max-orders-idUSKBN1X92D4

Boeing new about the potential flaw in the 737 Max. https://www.bbc.com/news/business-48174797#:~:text=Boeing%20has%20admitted%20that%t20it,did%20not%20jeopardise%20flight%20safety.

The FAA informed pilots the 737 Max had a "flight control system" that could cause pilots to have "difficulty controlling the airplane" and result in "possible impact with terrain." https://www.youtube.com/watch?v=djztRRaalOI

Pilots told Boeing, "We flat out deserve to know what is on our airplanes." https://www.youtube.com/watch?v=djztRRaalOI

Grounding the 737 Max, https://en.wikipedia.org/wiki/Boeing_737_MAX_groundings

The FAA admitted it never fully analyzed the MCAS system prior to certifying the 737 Max as fit for flight, https://www.nytimes.com/2019/07/27/business/boeing-737-max-faa.html

For additional articles on the 737 Max disaster, see, https://www.nytimes.com/2019/03/17/world/europe/boeing-737-ethiopian-black-box.html, https://www.businessinsider.com/ethiopian-airlines-et302-boeing-737-max-crash-timeline-2019-4#et302-was-the-second-nearly-brand-new-boeing-737-max-to-crash-in-a-matter-of-months-lion-air-flight-jt610-crashed-into-the-java-sea-on-october-28-under-eerily-similar-circumstances-13, https://en.wikipedia.org/wiki/Ethiopian_Airlines_Flight_302, https://www.youtube.com/watch?v=djztRRaalOI, https://www.youtube.com/watch?v=H2tuKiiznsY

Chapter 9: Forsee Failure

For the Unreal Deli pitch, see Shark Tank season 11, episode 8.

For the Mix Bikini story, see their Shark Tank pitch and the follow up on Beyond the Tank.

The World Health Organization reduces complications by instituting a checklist, https://www.who.int/teams/integrated-health-services/patient-safety/research/safe-surgery

David Bowie on Chris Hadfield, https://www.independent.co.uk/arts-entertainment/music/david-bowie-how-chris-hadfield-space-oddity-cover-orbit-was-helped-real-starman-a6805586.html

Most of the stories from Chris Hadfield are taken from his book, <u>An Astronaut's Guide to Life on Earth</u>.

Chapter 10: Protect Your Downside

Per Lindstrand's quote about dying if the balloon capsule lost pressure came from Richard Branson's autobiography, <u>Losing My Virginity</u>, pages 302-303. Many of the other Virgin stories also come from that book, as well as from Richard Branson's course on Masterclass.com.

See also https://en.wikipedia.org/wiki/Richard_Branson for details on the over 400 companies he's built.

Notes

"The best way of running a business is just to throw yourself in the deep end and learn all those things and ask lots of questions. Listen, listen, listen. And that's what I did when I was young." This Branson quote comes from his interview with Guy Raz on NPR's How I Built This, https://www.npr.org/2017/01/30/511817806/virgin-richard-branson

"If you are a risk taker, then the art is to protect the downside." Losing My Virginity page 131.

Virgin Atlantic filing for bankruptcy, https://www.theguardian.com/business/2020/aug/04/virgin-atlantic-files-for-bankruptcy-as-covid-continues-to-hurt-airlines#:~:text=Virgin%20Atlantic%20has%20filed%20for,in%20New%20York%20on%20Tuesday.&text=Virgin%20Australia%2C%20the%20country's%20second,to%20more%20than%2012%2C000%20creditors.

Chapter 11: Build Early Warning Systems

For information on the Time Warp Festival, see https://www.residentadvisor.net/news/34373, https://mixmag.net/read/time-warp-argentina-organizers-arrested-over-festival-casualties-news, https://www.independent.co.uk/news/world/europe/buenos-aires-nightclubs-face-closure-following-time-warp-festival-drug-deaths-a7008571.html, and https://www.talkingdrugs.org/uruguay-carries-out-first-ever-pill-testing-harm-reduction-initiative-at-festival

Chapter 12: Heed the Signs

For details on the Osirak nuclear reactor strike, see https://en.wikipedia.org/wiki/Operation_Opera and https://www.israeldefense.co.il/en/content/operation-opera-intelligence-behind-scenes

Escape velocity, see https://www.redshift-live.com/en/magazine/articles/Exploring_Space/8671-Rocket_speed-1.html and https://what-if.xkcd.com/58/

Satellites burn up on reentry, https://spaceplace.nasa.gov/spacecraft-graveyard/en/#:~:text=Two%20things%20can%20happen%20to,even%20farther%20away%20from%20Earth.&text=That%20way%2C%20it%20will%20fall,burn%20up%20in%20the%20atmosphere.

Foam strike on Colombia, https://www.space.com/19436-columbia-disaster.html, https://www.youtube.com/watch?v=aXiZ3RHR3bg, https://arstechnica.com/science/2016/02/the-audacious-rescue-plan-that-might-have-saved-space-shuttle-columbia/

Denial of requests to investigate for damage, https://www.youtube.com/watch?v=aXiZ3RHR3bg

Colombia destruction, see https://www.forbes.com/sites/quora/2017/02/03/why-is-it-so-difficult-for-a-returning-spacecraft-to-re-enter-our-atmosphere/#7592a9ac1177 and https://www.britannica.com/event/Columbia-disaster

Shuttle launches, see https://en.wikipedia.org/wiki/List_of_Space_Shuttle_missions

For a fantastic exploration on what could have been possible had NASA attempted a shuttle rescue, see https://arstechnica.com/science/2016/02/the-audacious-rescue-plan-that-might-have-saved-space-shuttle-columbia/

For the value of a human life, see https://www.npr.org/2020/04/23/843310123/how-government-agencies-determine-the-dollar-value-of-human-life

Apollo 13 episode, see https://en.wikipedia.org/wiki/Apollo_13#cite_ref-FOOTNOTENASA_197015_148-0

Chapter 13: Quit like a Champion

For Stewart Butterfield's story, see https://www.lovemoney.com/gallerylist/86993/slack-technologies-founder-billionaire-stewart-butterfield-net-worth-commune and https://www.npr.org/2018/07/27/633164558/slack-flickr-stewart-butterfield, https://en.wikipedia.org/wiki/Stewart_Butterfield

Glitch, see https://en.wikipedia.org/wiki/Slack_Technologies, https://www.glitchthegame.com/items/drinks/butterfly-milk/

Chapter 14: Own Your Failures

The <u>Dream, Design, Manifest</u> course mainly taught tools from our book, <u>The Size of Your Dreams</u>, available at https://thesizeofyourdreams.com

Chapter 15: Exceed Expectations

Learn more about Marie Forleo's B-School at https://www.marieforleo.com/bschool

Learn more about AppSumo at https://appsumo.com

Chapter 16: The Power of Belonging

See Traffic Secrets at https://www.amazon.com/Traffic-Secrets-Russell-Brunson-ebook/dp/B07M9HFLV6/ref=sr_1_1?keywords=traffic+secrets&qid=1683287684&sr=8-1

About the Author

Dave Mason is a novelist, strategic business coach, and investor.

He defines his mission as "Learn, Grow, Teach." He actively seeks opportunities to learn new things, grow from the lessons, and share that wisdom with others. His greatest wish is that you learn key lessons in this book, incorporate them into your life, and inspire others.

Dave helps businesses optimize and grow both as an owner/investor and as a strategic business coach. He's passionate about personal growth, healthy living, and transformational stories.

He lives with his wife Chana and son Aryeh Lev in the funky Nachlaot neighborhood of Jerusalem, where they interact with tourists, adventurers, and spiritual seekers from all over the world.

Connect with Dave at

DaveMasonAuthor.com/connect

Other books by Dave Mason

The Lamp of Darkness
www.theageofprophecy.com

The Key of Rain
www.theageofprophecy.com

The Size of Your Dreams
www.thesizeofyourdreams.com

The Cash Machine
www.buildmycashmachine.com

Did you enjoy Hurry Up and Fail?
Keep reading for a preview of
The Size of Your Dreams

Chapter One

The New Math

"*What is my goal in taking this class?*" Jarod Miller stared at the sheet in his hands, eyebrows shooting up. "What kind of math test is this?"

"I never called it a math test," Mr. Griffin said.

Trigonometry had been a disaster ever since Mr. Higgs suffered a stroke in late September. They'd transferred as many students as possible into Mrs. Northrup's class but had to stop when they hit the 30 student limit. During the weeks since, the school shuffled in a stream of substitutes, and most of the remaining students dropped out, leaving just four of us, all seniors. None of us knew where they dug up Mr. Griffin.

Despite there only being four of us left, Jarod moved right past me to the back of the room, because Jarod always sat in the back. His hair still had that just-got-out-of-bed rustle, though it was already fifth period. Stout and muscular, ahe could have been an athlete but gave up sports years ago when he gave up everything else school related. His main workouts now came behind a lawnmower or snow blower.

"Oh no!" Christy Mendez walked in and took a paper. "You're handing out a test? That's so unfair."

"Is there a problem, Christy?"

"You know my name?"

"Yes, I know all of your names." Mr. Griffin's piercing blue eyes caught each of ours. I couldn't help but look away. "Now the problem?"

"You haven't taught us anything yet."

The Size of Your Dreams

"Agreed. This is to make sure we change that."

Christy mouthed to Jarod, "you've got to be kidding me" and eased into the seat next to his. She eyed Mr. Griffin as she pulled her coffee-colored hair into a ponytail. Besides being captain of the girls' swim team, Christy studied harder than almost anyone. She was sizing up this new guy—she needed trig to get into college.

Darnell Jones lugged himself in, sweaty and winded, just as the bell rang. Jarod liked to joke that Darnell and Billy Jenks were playing a chess match to see who would graduate the fattest, with Billy playing the white pieces, and Darnell, one of only a handful of African Americans in school, playing the black. Darnell squeezed his oversized frame into the desk next to mine and tipped a quick nod in my direction.

"Whatever you call this paper, isn't the answer obvious?" Jarod asked.

"Is it, Jarod? Perhaps I've underestimated you. Today is, after all, my first day teaching. How about you go ahead and fill it out, and we'll see how obvious it is. Fifteen minutes should be enough."

Mr. Griffin sat atop one of the student desks, reading off some note cards and mumbling to himself. He was a surprisingly tall figure. Trimly cropped black hair topped his lean face. He wore a raven-black dress shirt and khakis that fell smoothly over his loafers. His legs pumped back and forth, showing off purple polka-dotted socks.

"Not looking good," Jarod whispered to Christy. "Even I can read without moving my lips."

It only took me a few seconds to answer the question. When I finished, everyone except Darnell had stopped writing. A moment later, his pencil hit the table as well.

Mr. Griffin was so immersed in his notecards, he didn't even notice we were all done. "Uh, Mr. Griffin?" I said.

He looked up from his cards. "Yes, Kelvin? Do you need me to clarify the assignment?"

"No. It's just…. We're all done."

"All of you?" He scanned the room. "Already?"

"Well, yeah," Darnell said. "The question was kind of easy."

"Was it? Personally, I consider it to be quite difficult. But pass back your papers. Let's see how you've all done."

Jarod grabbed Christy's and stretched forward to pass theirs up to me. With three rows of empty chairs between us, I still had to get up to take them. I grabbed Darnell's on my way back and handed all four to Mr. Griffin.

"Darnell," Mr. Griffin said, "you wrote that your goal this year is to learn trigonometry. Why is that important to you?"

The New Math

Darnell shrugged. "It's important stuff to know."

"Is it? Can you give me one example of how you anticipate using trigonometry later in your life?"

Darnell wiped his forehead with the back of his sleeve. "Uh..."

"Your homework, Darnell, will be to ask your parents what math skills they still use and try to ascertain in what grade they learned them. The answer might surprise you."

Mr. Griffin turned to my test. "Kelvin, your goal is to learn how to think better. Are you saying that trigonometry is like a game to test your mind?"

"Yeah, sort of," I said. "It helps you think analytically."

"And do you believe trigonometry is the most effective tool available for teaching analytical thinking? Do you find that math pushes you to your intellectual limits, Kelvin?"

"Not really. I usually get A's without trying too hard."

Jarod scoffed behind me.

"Oh leave him alone, Jarod," Christy said. "It may not come as easy for me as for Kelvin, but I'm also here to get an A."

"Indeed," Mr. Griffin said, "getting an A was what you listed as your goal. Why is that important to you?"

"I need to get a scholarship for college."

"Come on, Christy," Jarod said, "if you get a scholarship it's going to be for your swimming. You're better off working on your breaststroke."

"Grades can play a role too, especially at the better schools. Besides, now that coach is gone, I doubt my times will improve any."

"And you, Jarod?" Mr. Griffin said. "Care to share with the class what you wrote?"

"I'm here for one reason and one reason only. To graduate. I need one more math credit before they'll let me out of this place."

"So your goal in this class is just to get through it?"

"Pretty much."

"Well, it's nice to know that each of you has such low expectations," Mr. Griffin said. "That certainly takes pressure off me. I expect we can achieve most of that quite easily."

Low expectations? Collectively we'd said that we wanted to learn the subject matter, strengthen our thinking abilities, get good grades, and fulfill our educational requirements. What else were we in school for? I raised my hand, but didn't wait to be called on before saying, "What about you, Mr. Griffin? You seem unimpressed with our goals for the class. What are yours?"

The Size of Your Dreams

"I'm glad you asked, Kelvin." Mr. Griffin picked up a notecard from his desk and read:

> *My goal for my trigonometry class is to instill in my students a glimpse of the greatness they have within them and to provide tools to help them succeed in life: emotionally, physically, spiritually, and financially.*

"What the…" Jarod mumbled so quietly I couldn't hear the rest of his words. Darnell said, "Isn't one of your goals to teach us math?"

"Oh right, I should probably add that." Mr. Griffin grabbed a pen and wrote below his other goals. He then read out:

> *And get all students to master the State approved curriculum for this class.*

At this point, we were speechless. Mr. Griffin passed back our papers. "You all filled these out quite quickly the first time. Take the rest of today's class and tonight to rethink your answers. That will be your homework. Darnell, remember you have an additional assignment, to check with your parents regarding the math they use in their lives."

* * *

My 12-year-old sister Megan dragged her feet across the floor as she came in for dinner. Random strings of dirty-blond hair fluttered out of her braid.

"Everything okay at school, sweetie?" Mom placed her hand on Megan's shoulder, but she slunk out of reach.

"It was fine." My sister slid into her chair.

Mom served us chicken, peas, and mashed potatoes. I got a double serving of the mash, my favorite.

She turned to me. "How about you? How was school?"

"Fine. We finally got a new math teacher," I said, before shoving a forkful of chicken into my mouth.

"So perhaps you'll be able to learn trig this year, after all."

The New Math

"Maybe," I mumbled.

"You don't like him?"

"I dunno. He's kinda weird. I still wish I was in calculus this year."

"This again?" My father asked, glancing up from his research study. It was his fault that I was in trig this year rather than in calculus. When the rest of the advanced math class had gone on to trig last year, he insisted that I take Stats instead. "Statistics are key to understanding data, and data is everywhere. A recent study by the New England Journal of Medicine showed that 5 out of 4 doctors don't understand basic statistics, and they're supposed to be scientists." Dad grinned at his own joke. "You'll thank me for it one day."

I wasn't feeling too thankful at the moment, but I kept my mouth shut. As a neurobiology professor, Dad used statistics all the time in his work, so I couldn't deny their value. But had I taken trig with the rest of my class I could be in calculus now with a normal teacher, rather than stuck with Mr. Griffin.

"How is the new teacher weird?" Mom always broke in with a change of subject when Dad and I got to arguing.

"I dunno, Mom, just weird, okay?"

My mom, as usual, let the subject drop. Megan piped in, "Weird like you, maybe?"

"Shut up, Megan."

I was more curious about this new teacher than I let on to my family. That night I quickly worked through my homework for my other subjects, then dived into math. I didn't spend any time thinking over Mr. Griffin's idiotic question, though. No math teacher showed up the first day of class and forgot he was supposed to be teaching us math. There was something strange about this guy, and I intended to find out what it was.

The problem was, Griffin wasn't such an uncommon name, and teachers weren't known to leave deep digital footprints. Still, one of my counselors at Hacker Camp used to say that with enough skill and perseverance, you could find information on anyone. I'd been programming since before I could ride a bike, so no issue with my computer skills. And my parents almost never checked on me after I went to bed, so as long as I didn't make too much noise, I could stay up all night if I had to.

I had two computers in my room (one a Mac, the other an old PC that I'd converted to Linux) and a total of four monitors. I powered them all on and prepared to dig in. The school website didn't have him listed, but I found a notice on the Superintendent's site mentioning he'd been hired to take over Mr. Higgs' trigonometry class for the rest of the year. That was

The Size of Your Dreams

odd; I assumed he'd take over all of Mr. Higgs' classes, but it was just ours. More importantly, I got the piece of information I'd been looking for: his first name. It is far easier to search for people with unusual names—you don't get so many false positives. So when I saw that his first name was Mark, I knew I was out of luck.

I pulled up a digital notepad and typed in all I knew. It wasn't much. His name was far too common to be of much use. He was only part-time at the school and had just started teaching there, so he likely hadn't even updated his LinkedIn profile with the school name yet—if he even had one. He was teaching math, but this bizarre first day made me doubt he'd ever taught before, much less have a teaching degree. The one thing I felt confident about was location. He wouldn't commute more than 30 miles to get to some part-time teaching job. There were no more than ten towns within that radius, so I'd start by searching his name followed by each of the town names until I found all of the Mark Griffins living in this part of the state.

I dragged my notepad to my secondary monitor and opened a browser on my main one. Though I knew it was pointless, I started off with just the most general search, typing only his name into the search bar.

And there he was. Just like that. First page, first result. I knew it was the same Mark Griffin because Google posted a picture of him in the right column, along with a link to his Wikipedia page. His Wikipedia page? He must be the first teacher in the history of our school, perhaps the first teacher of *any* school, with his own Wikipedia page.

Ding. It was Darnell on chat.

"Hey," he wrote. "Some first day of math, eh?"

"No kidding. How are you doing?"

"Still reeling from last night's game. I can't believe I didn't start Gurley."

I didn't share Darnell's love of football, but I nonetheless let him talk me into joining his fantasy league. I hadn't even checked the scores yet this week. "He had a good game?"

"198 yards and two touchdowns. Man, I wish I could run like that."

As the fattest, slowest kid I knew, Darnell could barely run down the hall, much less a football field. I ignored his comment, and typed, "BTW, Mr. Griffin has his own Wikipedia page."

"No way!!!!" Darnell wrote. "Send me the link."

I copied and pasted it over, then dived into the article. Turns out he studied machine learning and artificial intelligence at MIT, the same school I was hoping to attend. Then he went to work building high-volume stock market trading machines for some investment bank I'd never heard of. He left after three years and began a data mining startup, apparently self-funding it with earnings from his banking job. Last year he sold the company to Oracle.

"It says he sold his business for some undisclosed amount," Darnell wrote. "How much do you think that is?"

"No clue, but enough that he doesn't need the salary from a part-time teaching job."

"So what's he doing here?"

"Your guess is as good as mine." I sent the link to Christy and Jarod, who despite not having much to do with me in school were still my Facebook "friends." I pulled out the "test" from math class where I'd written that my goal was "To learn how to think better." It was such an obvious answer at the time, though Mr. Griffin had been unimpressed.

As much as he seemed like a kook in class, everything I'd just learned about Mr. Griffin made me wonder, what should my answer be?

Chapter Two

The Power of Incentives

"You're staring." Wally elbowed my arm.

I'd just finished my sandwich, and my eyes had wandered over to Christy's table. Where Monica Gray sat. My attention quickly found its way back to the apple in my hand. "No, I'm not."

"Kelvin, who do you think you're kidding? She doesn't even know your name."

"Sure she does. We had lab together last year."

"You had lab with who?"

"Monica."

"You mean the girl you *weren't* staring at?" Wally slapped his leg and chortled. He was the only kid in school who could program as well as I could, and he always looked for opportunities to outsmart me.

"Ha ha," I said, wanting to bring the conversation to an end as quickly as I could. I also enjoyed one-upping Wally, and of the two of us, I had the sharper wit. But Monica was turning in our direction now. It was bad enough that my face was breaking out worse than ever today. Being seen hanging out with Wally Hoster, whose hair was so greasy he could shape it without gel, was enough to earn social exile. Mind, I was already sitting next to him, but that was just because it beat sitting alone. Barely.

"There's no point anyway." Bits of egg salad sprayed out of Wally's mouth as he spoke. "It's not like she's gonna follow you to MIT."

* * *

The Power of Incentives

When Jarod sat down in the second to last row, I knew my message about Mr. Griffin had piqued his interest. Christy sat in the desk in front of him. Even Darnell made a special effort to get to class before the bell, which left him sweatier than usual.

Mr. Griffin sat at his desk reading his notecards. When the bell rang, he put them down and stepped to the front of the class.

"Darnell, tell us about your homework."

Darnell was still huffing when he said, "I asked my folks what math they used, and the only things they could think of were addition, subtraction, multiplication, division, and fractions, all of which they learned by the 5th grade."

"Interesting. What do—?"

"Wait," he put up his hand, "there's more. Then I called my uncle. He couldn't think of any time he used advanced math either, but my aunt said she uses it in her job every day."

"And what does she do?"

Darnell grinned. "She's a high school math teacher."

Mr. Griffin raised an eyebrow. "So what do you take away from all of this?"

Darnell huffed out one final breath. "I'm mostly confused. Usually, teachers try to get us more interested in their subjects, you seem to want us to be less interested."

"Not at all. I just want you to understand the limitations of the curriculum alone."

I broke in. "The school must consider the curriculum valuable. Otherwise, they wouldn't require it."

Jarod scoffed. "The curriculum is like a hundred years old. It's not like they update it for the times."

"Don't discard something just because it's old," Mr. Griffin said. "The techniques I use every day are more than a hundred years old, and I've still never found anything more potent. Nonetheless, I agree that mastering the material in your classes is no longer the ticket to success or even employment that it once was."

"Does this mean you're not going to teach us math?" Christy asked.

"I've been hired to be your math teacher. Despite what others may think of my techniques, I always live up to my obligations. Speaking of which, I'd like hear how all of you expanded on yesterday's assignment."

I bit my lip. Despite my late-night efforts, I hadn't added a word to my page. Judging from the silence in the room, I wasn't alone.

After a painfully long delay, Mr. Griffin said, "I see." He slowly paced down one of the empty aisles of the classroom, rolling a pen between his fingers.

When he reached the last desk, he punctured the air with the pen. "I've got it. I know why you're all struggling to put effort into yesterday's assignment."

"Because it's ridiculously easy?" Jarod suggested.

"No, because it's ridiculously hard. It was unfair of me to give you such a task on day one. Indeed, I see now that I violated one of my core principles."

"Which is what?" Christy asked.

"To always start with vision. I tried, but I defined my question far too narrowly to get you there."

Jarod stretched his hands out before him and moved them around an imaginary orb. Speaking with the thick accent of a fortune teller at a fair, he said, "I envision passing trigonometry so I can get out of this school."

"Precisely," Mr. Griffin said. "All you want to do is leave school because you have no compelling vision of what you want to get from school."

Jarod's hands dropped. He stared back, silent.

"Does that mean," Darnell said, "that you want to change the question from what we hope to get out of trigonometry to what we hope to get out of school?"

"No, no, no Darnell, it's still too narrow. How can you know what you want to get out of school without first knowing what you want out of life?"

Mr. Griffin was practically bouncing, but I couldn't share his enthusiasm.

"I totally know what I want to do," Christy said. "I want to become a physical therapist."

"Very good. If you know what you want to do for a living, you're already ahead of most. But I don't just want a vision for your job—I want a vision for your *life*. That includes a vision for your home, family, and community. For how you spend time *outside* of work, not just *in* it."

"Ugh." Christy rolled her eyes and crossed her arms. "Why is it that whenever a woman brings up career, the automatic response is that she has to think about family?"

"As a woman, it's more likely that you've at least given it some thought," Mr. Griffin said. "Most men never give family a moment's consideration until it's too late."

"How's it ever too late?" Darnell asked.

Mr. Griffin sighed. "I can't tell you how many of my peers spent a fortune in tuition and years of their lives pursuing careers that only lasted two or three years because they suddenly had a family and found their jobs incompatible."

Christy's arms unclenched.

I thought about my own plans. I always dreamed of working for some hard-core start-up. The programmers I met who'd gone down that path didn't just work 80 hour weeks, they bragged about it. Somehow, I'd never given any thought to having a family at the same time. Did I really want to have kids but never see them?

"So how am I supposed to get a vision for my life?" Darnell asked.

"Here's a very simple exercise. Close your eyes. Go on Jarod—I'm not going to throw anything at you. Good. Take three slow, deep breaths."

My body sank deeper into my seat.

Mr. Griffin's voice grew softer. "Now, imagine yourself twenty years in the future. You're happy. Life has been good to you. You feel tremendously grateful that everything has fallen into place. Look around you."

"All I see is an empty math class," Jarod said.

"Eyes closed, Jarod. I want you to visualize your future. What does your life look like?" He paused. I immediately saw an image of working at a startup. "Are you married?"

My initial thought was yes, but I couldn't envision that.

"Do you have children? Where do you live? What do you do? How do you contribute to others?" The questions came faster now, and while visions flashed across my mind, I couldn't hold all of them. "Open your eyes, and write down what you saw."

Mr. Griffin paced back to his chair, sat down, and propped his heels up on his desk. He pulled a tattered book out of his briefcase. I tilted my head to get a look at the cover. *Think and Grow Rich*. He opened to a dog-eared page in the middle of the tome and said, "You have until the end of class."

The first thing I wrote about was my career. That part was easy. I knew I wanted to create world-changing technologies. Like Tesla. Not Tesla now, with its billions of dollars in income, but like Tesla when they first started out.

As to where I'd live, that was also easy. There were really only a few options for that type of work. Silicon Valley, Seattle, Austin. I'd put down Austin for now; it was more up and coming.

That's when I got stuck. *Marriage? Children? Community?*

I put down my pen and looked around the class. Mr. Griffin was still absorbed in his book. Christy was bent over her paper, had already written a full page, and was still going strong. Jarod was leaning back, playing with his Leatherman. His sheet of paper was glaringly white for its blankness. Darnell had his pen close to the top of his page and was staring up at the ceiling, looking for answers.

I returned to my own paper. *Why was this so difficult?* Not a day went by when I didn't think about having more friends, and hardly an hour when I didn't think about having a girlfriend. That's really all Mr. Griffin had asked us to do, to think about what we wanted in life. So why was I all of a sudden drawing a blank?

The Size of Your Dreams

* * *

The next morning, I dragged myself out of bed and moved through the house like a soggy mop. My mother eyed me all through breakfast, but she knew better than to ask me questions that early in the day. Megan read her Kindle while she ate, paying me no mind.

I had flitted in and out of sleep the night before, haunted by a recurring dream about living at some high-tech start-up with a blow-up mattress, a nightlight, and a teddy bear stored under my cubicle desk. I spent dark, cold nights there alone with only microwave pizza to keep me company. Everything felt so incredibly normal, but I woke up in sweats each time the microwave beeped that the pizza was ready. Was this my future?

I had a hard time keeping my eyes, or even my mind, open during the first few hours of the day. By the time fifth period came around, I was ready to crawl into the janitor's closet and use *his* mop as a pillow. Beside my exhaustion was the uneasy feeling that I'd have to revisit my nightmare during Mr. Griffin's class. Plus, I hadn't completed his assignment. I never did that.

"Okay, what have you all got?" Mr. Griffin said as soon as we were all seated. "Jarod?"

"This assignment was lame." The thick rubber soles of his work-boots drummed against the leg of his desk. "What kinda math class is this anyhow?"

"Lame," Mr. Griffin said. "I see…So, you don't have any plans for your future?"

"Just the same crap as everyone else. College, job, wife, kids, house, retire, die. What's there to write?"

Mr. Griffin looked at the rest of us. "You all have something like this?"

"More or less…," Christy's shoulders rose to meet her ears. She'd written a hundred times more than Jarod and ten times more than I had. Did everything she jotted down really get summed up by Jarod in just a few words? Mine didn't even get that far.

"I thought our visions were pretty lame," Jarod said, "but you seem mighty impressed."

Mr. Griffin indeed was practically bouncing at the front of the class. "Impressed? Hardly. I'm excited by their very lameness."

"You like lame?" Christy asked.

"Absolutely. It tells me that, like most people, you've never given much thought to your life goals."

"And that's good?" I asked.

"For me it is. I don't teach for the benefits, and certainly not for the salary.

The Power of Incentives

I'm here because I want to create lasting change. Frankly, I'm new at this. I had no idea how easy or hard this would be. But now that I see you've all set the bar so low, I do not doubt that I can completely revolutionize your lives this year."

Mr. Griffin may have been grinning from ear to ear, but we couldn't share his enthusiasm. Was he really telling us all that we were pathetic and mindless? And this was *good* news because he was going to somehow fix us?

"You still didn't answer my question." Jarod kicked the legs of his desk. "What does this have to do with math?"

"If I do my job well, you'll find within yourself the ability to go as far as you want with your mathematics. Nonetheless, my core goal as your teacher is not confined to math."

Christy leaned forward in her chair. "So what is your goal?"

"My goal is to activate your minds, to give you the tools to succeed no matter what direction you take."

If I hadn't read the article on him the other night, I wouldn't have given his words much credence. But this guy was no stranger to success.

Jarod, however, was more interested in what it would cost him. "You're going to do this by the end of the year, *on top* of teaching us math? Just how much homework do you plan on giving us?"

"Five minutes a day."

"Five minutes? That's it?"

"That's all it will take to implement my basic techniques. Beyond that, I expect you'll each want to push yourselves to do more. But those will be *your* steps toward *your* goals, not mine."

"What are these techniques?" I asked. "You said they were a hundred years old?"

"If you dig deep enough, you'll find variations in use even thousands of years ago. But the first time I know they were written down was in 1937."

"Who wrote them?"

"Napoleon Hill."

Jarod scoffed. "That French dude?"

Christy slapped his shoulder. "That was Napoleon Bonaparte. We just learned about him in European history last year. Where were you?"

"Who's Napoleon Hill?" I asked.

Mr. Griffin sat on his desk. "Ever heard of Andrew Carnegie?"

"As in Carnegie Hall?" Christy asked.

"Wasn't he a Robber Baron?" I asked.

"You're both right. He started out as a penniless immigrant, working twelve hour days for $1.20 a week. He worked his way up to become one of

The Size of Your Dreams

the wealthiest men in the world, then spent the latter portion of his life giving most of it away. He built Carnegie Hall as well as countless libraries around the world."

"What does he have to do with this Napoleon guy?" Darnell asked.

"Carnegie gave the young Napoleon Hill a task, and Hill spent the next 25 years completing it."

"What was the task?" I asked.

"To study the elements of success."

"So he studied successful people?" I asked.

"Not only. It wasn't enough to find commonalities among the successful. He also had to find what distinguished them from those he deemed failures."

"Those notecards you read," Jarod nodded to the cards next to Mr. Griffin. "They come from him?"

"They're my own practice, but I developed them by applying the principles I learned from Napoleon Hill."

"Let me guess," Jarod kicked his desk extra hard. "You want to fix our goals, and then I suppose you'll have us write them down on notecards?"

Mr. Griffin grinned like the Cheshire cat. "No, I want *you* to fix your goals." He leaned in toward Jarod. "We'll go over the steps of creating truly compelling goals for your life, as well as how to reinforce them so that they stick. That's where the notecards come in."

"How do they work?" Darnell asked. Was he actually excited by this?

"There are three components of the Outcome Cards. The first is your goal, the second is your deadline, and the third is the list of steps you'll take to hit that goal."

"Can you give us an example?" Darnell asked again.

"Certainly." Mr. Griffin picked up his stack of notecards, pulled one out and read:

> I intend to bring my marathon time down to three hours and fifteen minutes or below by April 16, in time for the Boston Marathon. To do this, I will 1) run at least four days per week, 2) run at least a half-marathon distance every Sunday, 3) weight train on my non-running days, 4) reward myself each time I break my fastest time, and 5) book additional training sessions with my coach whenever my average time drops.

"You run marathons?" Christy asked.

"I'm starting to. I want to compete in Ironman as well, but one thing at a time."

"So you're just supposed to let this piece of paper dictate what you do?" Jarod asked.

Mr. Griffin walked straight to Jarod's desk and slapped his notecard down on it. "Who wrote the note, Jarod?"

"I guess you did."

"And who developed the steps on the card?"

"Looks like the same handwriting to me…"

"Good to see you're paying attention," Mr. Griffin said. "So, who is dictating to whom?"

"I get your point, but still…." Jarod flicked his hand in the air. "It's like school — just having to follow more directions. Why should you have a notecard at all? Can't you just do what you want without it?"

"Yes, but I'm hardly consistent. Some days I want one thing, other days it's something else. That's why most people make such little progress in their lives. They never build momentum."

"This is ludicrous," Christy said. "Say one day I think I want to study law, and the next day I change my mind to medicine. You're saying that because I wrote law down on the notecard that I should stick with it?"

"Truthfully Christy, how often do you waffle between two burning desires?"

Christy shifted in her chair. "It happens sometimes."

"If you have even one burning desire, you're well ahead of the pack. Most people simply focus on getting through the day, the week, the semester, or whatever it is. To use your example, you'd be more likely to waffle between a vague idea that you'd sort of like to study law and another vague idea that you kinda think medicine would be better."

Jarod picked up Mr. Griffin's card and flapped it back and forth before him. "And these notecards are supposed to change that?"

"Absolutely. The present moment is like twilight. The past behind you is bright and clear, but the future ahead is a masked in darkness. Making an Outcome Card is like shining a beam of light into that darkness."

"You're telling me this card is going to predict my future?" Jarod asked.

"Your future is not set — there are infinite possibilities before you. The card helps you hone in on the future you choose to pursue."

"What if we make the card at the wrong time?" Darnell asked.

"What do you mean, the wrong time?"

"Well, like Christy said, sometimes you want law, other times medicine. What if you make the notecard during a time when you're thinking law, but you're better suited to medicine?"

"Excellent question, Darnell. That's why we make the cards during times of clarity."

"Like when?" Christy asked.

"Clarity most often comes at the extremes: when you're on top of the world and want to stay there, or when you hit rock bottom and want to pick yourself up. The problem is that these moments are fleeting."

"So we make the cards to remind us of the goals we made during those times of clarity?" I asked.

"Exactly. Then they keep us on track during the blah moments. For me, sometimes I want to train for the marathon; other times I'd rather sit on the couch with a beer and watch football. The notecards may be my voice, but they're my voice of vision. Any time that I think of skipping my workout, I read my card, and it's like my higher-self whispering in my ear."

"But isn't it possible," I asked, "that you can have a moment of clarity and still be wrong? Can't you have a rock bottom moment, say when you're struggling in biology, and suddenly see that it would be so much better to study law. What happens if you make my notecard and law isn't for you after all? Maybe you're best off sticking it through with medicine, or switching to engineering?"

"The notecards help you clarify that as well. Just because you write them doesn't mean that you're stuck with them for life. When I read my cards, I normally hear the voice of my higher-self. I know the goals on my card are what I want, and reading them helps me to refocus my energy. But periodically, when I read a card the goal doesn't move me at all. I don't hear the voice of my higher-self, I hear only delusion."

"What do you do then?" Christy asked.

"I tear up the card."

Christy's brow creased. She'd never given up on anything. "Just like that?"

"Normally I'll wait a day or two to make sure the feeling is consistent. Otherwise, I'd be in danger of trashing all my goals every time I get into a bad mood. But if nothing shifts, I tear it up."

Darnell picked at his cuticles, something he usually did during tests. "So if you keep not liking what the card says, you know you've set the wrong goal?"

"Or the wrong steps or the wrong date. Once you learn how to interpret your emotional reactions, they'll guide you toward your true goals as well as the ideal path to manifest them."

The Power of Incentives

* * *

The next day, we rehashed our questions from the day before, even though we knew the answers. I wasn't the only one still trying to get my head around the concept. One thing that had become clear, Mr. Griffin said, "is that you guys aren't ready to work on a greater vision for your lives. At this point, it's best to choose one small goal to focus on."

Late in the class, Jarod raised his hand. "Mr. Griffin, perhaps if there were some grade incentives tied to the cards it would help us try them out."

"Grade incentives?" Mr. Griffin asked.

Darnell perked up. "Yeah, like if we got an automatic A in math if we made these cards and stuck to them."

Mr. Griffin raised his eyebrows. "For the opportunity to help you get your life on track, I have to give you an automatic A?"

Jarod said, "It doesn't have to be an A. but an incentive would certainly help us stick to it."

The bell rang. "I'll think your idea over, Jarod. See you all tomorrow."

"Remind me, what were we talking about yesterday?" Mr. Griffin asked with a grin as we took our seats the next day.

"Grade incentives," Jarod said. "You said you'd think them over."

"And I did. Do you really feel that an incentive would help you make and stick to the cards?"

"Yes," Jarod said.

"Does everyone feel this way?"

The rest of us said, "Yes."

"It's not enough to just read them in math class. The most important times to read your cards are first thing in the morning to set your intentions for the day, and immediately before bed, so they truly penetrate your unconscious mind. To see their effectiveness, you'll have to commit to doing this for at least 30 days. Are you all willing to do that?"

We all said, "Yes."

"The problem is, how will I know if you've done them? If there's a grade incentive, then there's also an incentive to lie."

"We can use an app," I suggested. "Each time we read our card, we check off the app. You'll get a notice with the time we did it."

"Interesting idea, Kelvin, but what if one of you claims you read the card but forgot to check off the app?"

Christy said, "We can put a note on the bottom of our cards saying 'check off the app.' Then if there's no check on the app, you'll know we didn't do it."

"Does everyone agree that if the app does not report that you read off the card, you won't get credit for reading it that time?" Mr. Griffin asked.

We agreed.

"Very well. I found an app that would work last night. I'll send you the link after class."

"Wait," I said. "You already thought about an app?"

"Once you brought up grade incentives, it made sense to have a way to keep track."

"Then why didn't you tell us about it?"

"I'm not here to give you answers, but to help you work them out. Didn't it feel better to come up with the solution on your own?"

I was annoyed at his ploy but had to admit that it had felt good when I made the suggestion. "I suppose great minds think alike."

"In my experience, it's the opposite," Mr. Griffin said. "Extraordinary minds are original. Ordinary minds think alike. Or perhaps I should say that those who don't actively grow their minds think alike, for every human mind can be extraordinary."

Was he calling me ordinary? Or insinuating that I wasn't growing my mind?

"Does this mean you'll do the grade incentives?" Jarod asked.

"I'm willing to give them a shot. But on two conditions. One, I'm only going to offer them to those students who genuinely feel the grade incentives will help them. Intrinsic motivation always trumps incentives in my mind. But I will give it as a tool for those who need it. How many of you feel you need this?"

At this point, I was already curious to try out the cards. While I understood his point about intrinsic motivation, I wasn't dumb enough to turn down a grade incentive. I eagerly raised my hand with the rest of the class.

"Fine. It can apply to all of you. Second, I will only do it for students who will commit, right now, that once you have a card, you will read it twice a day for 30 days. Even though you don't have your cards yet, once you commit, there is no backing out. Whoever doesn't wish to commit can still participate at their own pace, but will not qualify for the grade incentives. Who is ready to commit right now?"

Again, all of us raised our hands.

"Very well, then I have a contract for you all to sign. Get in line and sign one by one."

Mr. Griffin brought out a bunch of papers from his desk. "I've already signed my name and dated these. You just need to sign and print your names below."

The pages he held were full of text, written in what looked like 8 point font.

The Power of Incentives

Darnell got up to the desk first and signed his name in the tiny space between the end of the text and the bottom of the page. I was next. The text began, "This is a contract between Mr. Griffin (herein "Mr. Griffin" or "teacher") and the students in his fifth-period trigonometry class (herein "student" or "students")…"

It would take me a full ten minutes to read the entire thing; maybe more, as it seemed all written in legalese. Sensing Jarod's impatience behind me, I quickly signed my name at the bottom as Darnell had. Neither Jarod nor Christy wasted their time with even trying to read over the text, just signed and returned to their seats.

Darnell seemed particularly pleased. "This is going to be the easiest math class ever! I can't believe I get an A for just reading this notecard twice a day."

"An A?" Mr. Griffin placed the signed contracts in a drawer, locked it, and dropped the key in his pocket. "That wasn't the agreement."

"Sure it was," Darnell said. "We talked about it yesterday."

"You suggested that yesterday. But the grade incentives weren't your idea—they were Jarod's. He was clear that the incentive didn't have to be an automatic A."

"So I'll still have to study math?" Darnell asked. "Bummer. But at least it should help. What do I get, another ten points on my average or something?"

"You don't get anything, Darnell. You lose points if you don't follow through."

"Lose points?" Jarod said. "That wasn't our deal."

"Of course it was. It was written very clearly on the contract you all signed."

"But we didn't even read the contracts."

"I noticed. Would you like to read them now?" Mr. Griffin handed around unsigned contracts, keeping the signed ones safely locked in his desk.

"Wait." Christy's eyes bulged over her copy. "I lose five points on my overall grade every time I forget to read my card?"

"Even if you remember to read the card, but forget to check the app," Mr. Griffin said. "Remember, that was your suggestion."

Heat rose to my cheeks. "If we forget more than five times we fail math?"

"Correct. Remember, I only gave this option to those who asked for a grade incentive. I always prefer intrinsic motivation. But you thought this would help you, so I offered it as a tool."

"A tool?" I said. "It sounds more like a punishment."

"Punishments, or the threat of them, can be great tools. You're all old enough to drive. How many of you try to stay within the speed limit?"

Silence.

"How many of you regularly go more than 20 miles per hour over the speed limit?"

Jarod raised his hand.

"The rest of you, what keeps you from driving that fast?"

"Over 20 miles an hour the tickets are like $160," Christy said.

"Yeah," Darnell said, "and my dad would take away my driving privileges if he ever caught me going that fast."

"None of you reduce your speed out of concern for safety?" Mr. Griffin asked.

No one responded.

"Teenagers." Mr. Griffin shook his head. "Do you see why society holds the threat of punishment over your heads? That's how they keep the roads safe."

A teacher intentionally tricking us into signing an agreement not in our interests? Who does this guy think he is? "I don't think it was fair putting it on the contract and not telling us," I said.

"Kelvin, do you remember what I told you my goals were for this year?"

I clenched my jaw and mumbled, "Something about helping us lead extraordinary lives."

"Precisely. Fairness was not among my goals."

We all groaned.

"Let this be a lesson to you. You must think hard about what you put on your cards because they'll give you laser focus toward these goals. Elements left off of your cards can get squeezed out." Mr. Griffin sat back on his desk. "Like fairness in my case."

"So now we're stuck?" Darnell asked.

"No, you're not stuck."

Darnell sat straighter. "You mean you'll let us take the contracts back?"

"No. That's another lesson I wanted to teach in a way that you'd never forget. You'll each sign hundreds, if not thousands of contracts in your life. Those who give them to you will primarily be looking out for their interests, not yours. Always be aware of what you bind yourself to."

Darnell's eyebrows pinched. "But you said we're not stuck?"

"You're not. You're welcome to transfer to another math class or drop math altogether. It all goes back to your vision for your life, and who you think can best help you get there. Care to transfer, Darnell?"

Darnell exhaled loudly. "No, I'll stay here."

"Anyone else?"

So far, I really couldn't say that I *liked* Mr. Griffin—he was like a mosquito that kept buzzing in my ear. Yet, he was intriguing. I doubted he'd ever bring us to the profound life transformations he promised, but no other teacher had ever attempted to. And…what if he did? Images of my nightmare in the cubicle wafted through my mind. My future vision could use some refining. It was worth a shot.

The Power of Incentives

When no one said they wanted to transfer, Mr. Griffin said, "Just remember that you're not trapped. You're choosing to stay here."

"I still feel stuck to this contract," Darnell said.

"Yes, I know. It's written in your posture. The more ownership you take over your decisions, the straighter you'll sit in your chair. Besides, being stuck is not the worst thing. Sometimes I intentionally get myself stuck."

"Why would you do that?" I asked.

"I do it for motivation, and to force myself to find new answers."

"How can getting stuck motivate you?" Christy asked.

"It's like when Cortez burnt his ships upon landing in Mexico in 1519. The message to his men was clear. You can't back out. Succeed or die. I've used that technique on myself, though with less dire consequences."

"Like when?" Christy asked.

"I used it in college when trying to lose weight."

Darnell's head tilted up. "You, lose weight?" He scanned our lean, muscular teacher with cold eyes.

"You might not guess it looking at me now," Mr. Griffin patted his stomach, "but I used to be over 100 pounds overweight."

"Really?" Darnell was easily that overweight himself. "How did you lose it?"

"I tried diet after diet. I must have lost the same five pounds ten times, but I always put them right back on."

"So how'd you keep them off?"

"I backed myself into a corner. I made sure that I had two options, weight loss or a fate far worse than hunger."

"Like what?" Darnell asked.

"I made a list of all the foods I knew I needed to avoid, and I gave a copy of the list to all of my friends, plus a few people who were anything but my friends. I told them all that if they caught me eating anything on that list, they could make me eat whatever they wanted."

"Anything?"

"Anything that wouldn't injure or kill me. One day I was walking with my friend Andres, and we passed some fresh dog poop on the ground next to a hamburger stand. Andres asked them for a paper plate and a spoon, and scooped the poop onto the plate." Mr. Griffin cringed. "He waved it in front of me, telling me how much fun he was going to have watching me eat it all."

"Gross!" Jarod pretended to puke behind his desk.

"You never did, did you?" Christy asked.

"No. I lost the pounds, and Andres wound up with stale dog poop in his fridge. A couple of times I came close to cheating, and each time all I had to do was think of that plate of dog poop. Just knowing it was there, waiting for me, was enough to keep me on my diet."

The bell rang.

"I trust you've all had a memorable day. Next week we'll start working on your cards. And don't worry. The 30 days haven't even started yet."

"When do they start?" Christy asked.

"Everything will be just like it says on your contract."

"Where?"

Mr. Griffin's smirk returned. "On the other part you didn't read."

Chapter Three

Sink or Swim

I was curled up on the couch reading *The Martian* and trying to avoid thinking about Mr. Griffin and his sleazy contract when Dad walked in. He wore the same old khaki pants and a wrinkled button-down shirt. At least he didn't have acne anymore, though the pockmarks on his face showed that his skin had looked just like mine back in the day.

"Hi Kelvin," he said.

I didn't even look up. "Hey."

"How was school?"

"Fine."

"Liking the new math teacher any more?"

I didn't want to go there. "Eh."

"So…a physicist from London is lecturing at the university about black holes next Friday evening. Want to go?"

While half the senior class was at some party? "Nah."

"You'll be sure to get sucked in."

It took all my strength not to roll my eyes.

"I don't need to know until late in the week. You think about it until then, okay Kelvin?"

"Sure, Dad."

I felt him standing by the doorway, stalling. I guess Dad couldn't think of anything else to say, because after a minute, he continued on towards the kitchen.

The Size of Your Dreams

* * *

"How about you, Christy. You have something you'd like to work on?"

It was Monday afternoon. Mr. Griffin just got through explaining the "rules." Each of us would start our 30 day period as soon as we chose our goal. He didn't want us to wait too long, or else we'd lose out on precious time. One goal immediately came to my mind, but there was no way I was going to discuss it in front of the class. When asked, I just lied and said I couldn't think of anything. Fortunately, Mr. Griffin moved on to Christy to find his first sucker.

"No, I don't have anything," Christy said.

"Nothing?"

"Nah. I had one, but I gave up on it."

"What was that?" Mr. Griffin asked.

"Last year, when coach appointed me captain of the girls' swim team, I made it my goal to win the State Championship this year."

"Why'd you give up on it?"

"You didn't hear what happened?"

Mr. Griffin rubbed his chin. "Was that the drunk driver?"

Christy nodded and tears collected in her eyes. "Coach was killed the week before school began."

"They haven't given you anyone else?"

"No." Christy shoved her hands into the narrow gap between her crossed legs. "I approached the athletic director, and he said he didn't have the time to get someone new. I learned later that they used most of the budget to get an extra assistant coach for the football team."

"Don't they legally have to give you a coach?"

"Yeah. There's this lady who works as a pool attendant who said she'd be willing to accompany us to meets, so he gave her a tiny salary and appointed her as our official coach. She doesn't do anything though."

"So who runs practice?"

"Jill and I. Jill is my co-captain. But we don't know what we're doing. The older girls aren't making any progress, and the younger ones are completely lost."

Mr. Griffin leaned on the edge of his desk. "Tell me about your coach."

"Coach Silver was amazing. When she made me captain and told me she wanted to win States this year, I actually thought we had a chance."

"And now?"

Christy shook her head. "Now we're hopeless."

Mr. Griffin swept his eyes over the entire class. "You get what you settle for."

Christy's eyes narrowed. "What does that mean?"

"You probably think that you gave up on your goal because it went out of reach. I expect it's the opposite: your goal left your reach because you gave up on it."

"Our coach died!" Christy's tears spilled down her cheeks. Why was Mr. Griffin being so heartless?

"Did you only want to win for the coach?" he asked.

Christy mumbled, "Of course not. For all of us."

"Then why give up just because you lost your coach?"

"We're not giving up. We're just hopeless." A new rush of anguish overcame her.

"*Hopeless*. An interesting choice of language. You didn't say you're incapable. After all, you have the same athletes on the team that you had before your coach died, so if you had the physical capabilities to win before, you've still got them now. As you point out, what's changed is your belief in yourselves. You no longer have hope."

"What's changed," Christy sat up straight and drove her words like daggers, "is that our coach is dead! We're lost without her."

Mr. Griffin kept his cool. "I'm not saying that your path is without challenges. But after all, there's little thrill in achieving easy victories. My goal is to stretch you, to show you that you're capable of achieving so much more than you realize."

"I know what the team is capable of, Mr. Griffin, and the championship is beyond us."

Mr. Griffin sighed and went to the whiteboard. "I want you all to remember this quote." He wrote down:

The Size of your Dreams must always exceed your current capacity to achieve them.
—Ellen Johnson Sirleaf

"Who is she?" Christy asked.

"The first woman ever elected President of an African nation. She also said, 'If your dreams do not scare you, they are not big enough.' She would know about scary dreams. Her efforts to end Liberia's cycle of violence and promote women's rights earned her a Nobel Peace Prize."

"Not all of us are looking to change the world, Mr. Griffin," Christy said.

"Big changes evolve from small changes, Christy. Today, we might only be working on a high school swim team, but you never know what challenge tomorrow brings. Master these tools now, and you'll be prepared to face whatever lies ahead."

The Size of Your Dreams

Christy sank into her chair and crossed her arms.

Mr. Griffin put down the whiteboard marker. "I know you're all deeply skeptical of my approach. Tell me, Christy, if following my steps leads you to win the State Championship, will I win you over to my methods?"

Christy's head bent to the side. "You serious?"

"You bet. If you won the Championship, would you trust me then?"

"Absolutely."

"I believe it's possible, but only if you're willing to try."

Christy shrugged her shoulders. "I'll try. Why not? You'll fail me anyhow if I don't."

"No, not like that. I'm not talking about putting a toe in the water. I'm talking about going all in, giving me everything you've got."

"I thought you said this was going to only be five minutes a day for 30 days?"

"That's right, your homework from me will only be five minutes a day for 30 days, but I need your complete dedication during those five minutes. Plus, you'll give yourself additional tasks to complete *your* goal. You'll need to put the same dedication into those. Agreed?"

"Okay, I guess."

"This is not a guessing game, Christy. Remember, you get what you settle for. Winning is going to take more dedication than that."

She wiped her eyes with the back of her hands. "I'm dedicated."

Mr. Griffin shook his head. "I don't know. I'm not seeing a girl who's passionate about winning the State Championship."

"What?" Christy slapped her hand against her desk. "How can you say that?"

"You think you have the passion it takes?"

"Absolutely."

"Then if you have the passion and the dedication, come up here."

Christy stepped up to the front of the room.

"Face the class and close your eyes. Go on, no one's going to laugh at you. Good. Now ask yourself, what would it mean to you to lead your team to victory in the State Championship?"

"It would be great."

"Just great? I want you to imagine that you've made it to the Championship and it's neck and neck. What's the last event?"

"The 4 x 100 relay."

"What place are you swimming?"

"Last, I'm the anchor."

"Excellent. So you're standing on the edge of the pool, waiting your turn. The girls on your team are good, but the competition is better. To your left and right, the anchors from the other teams jump into the pool. Finally, your teammate hits the edge of the pool, and you jump in. You're behind, but determined. By the time you finish your first lap, you've caught up to all but two of the swimmers. 50 yards to go. You're halfway through the second lap when you pass the next girl. 25 yards. You're tired. Your arms are burning. But nothing's going to stop you. You draw strength from deep down. 15 yards. She's still ahead. 10 yards. You're getting close. 5 yards. You've pulled even. You reach out and, by a finger's breath, hit the edge of the pool first.

"Can you see it, Christy?"

Christy nodded.

"Can you feel it, Christy?"

"Yes."

"What happens next?"

"The entire team goes crazy. They all jump into the pool and hug me. We're all screaming, some even crying." Christy's eyes swelled.

Mr. Griffin said, "You barely have time to towel off before someone hands you the largest trophy you've ever seen and a microphone. What do you say?"

"I'd take the trophy over to the stands."

"Why? Who's in the stands?"

"Coach Silver's nine-year-old daughter Kim is there, watching with her dad. I'd say, 'we want you to have this, Kim, from all the girls on the team. Whenever you look at it, we want you to remember everything your mom did for us. Without her, we never could have won. And remember all that she did for you. You didn't have her long enough. But with the gifts she gave you, you can do anything!"

"I want everyone to remember this look on Christy's face. That's the look of inspiration. With the expression she had ten minutes ago, she was barely capable of achieving the ordinary. With this look, she's ready to take on the *extraordinary*. Christy, make the sound of victory you're feeling right now."

Christy raised her eyebrows and shook her head.

"Come now, Christy. You told me you were fully dedicated."

She turned away and wiped her eyes.

Mr. Griffin faced us. "One reason that so few people achieve the extraordinary is that we get embarrassed by the power of our own greatness. Don't let Christy fall into that trap. If you believe in her, let her know."

Jarod, who never minded making an ass of himself in class, pumped his fist and started chanting, "Christy! Christy!"

Darnell and I looked at each other. I shrugged and joined in. Darnell threw

The Size of Your Dreams

his fist in the air. Ordinarily, teachers quieted us down when we started getting too rowdy, but Mr. Griffin screamed, "Louder!"

"Christy! Christy!"

"Don't let her stand there alone. If you believe in her, get on your feet."

Jarod was the first to rise. This math class was finally jiving with him. Once he was up, Darnell and I also stood up. "Christy! Christy!"

"You see, Christy," Mr. Griffin said, "you can't embarrass yourself in front of them. They're all behind you. They all believe in you. Now, let me hear the sound of victory."

Christy thrust her arms high, "Yeah!"

"Do it again. Louder"

"Yeaaaaaaaah!"

"Once again, but this time, I want everyone who believes in Christy to join in. Go!"

We all shouted. Jarod took her in a bear hug. When he let go, Darnell stepped forward, with arms halfway out, then backed off, hovering just beyond her reach.

"Now stop," Mr. Griffin said.

The class grew quiet.

"Everyone take your seats. That was the easy part."

Easy?

"Tell me, Christy, what would you do to make that vision a reality?"

"Anything."

"Anything? Be careful what you commit to. To get you there, we may have to put that 'anything' to the test."

Christy nodded. "What do I do now?"

"First, take a notecard. You're going to create what I call an Outcome Card." Mr. Griffin handed her one from his desk. "Write on the top:

> *I intend to captain the girls' swim team to Victory in the State Championship on...*

"When's the championship?"

"March 8th."

> *I intend to captain the girls' swim team to victory in the State Championships on March 8th. To accomplish this, I will do the following:*

198

"Got it," Christy looked up. "What do I write next?"

"I have no idea," Mr. Griffin said.

"That's all that goes on the card?"

"No. You need to write down the steps you'll take."

"What are the steps?" Christy asked.

"How should I know?" Mr. Griffin shrugged. "I don't know what it takes to win at swimming. I can't even do the backstroke."

"You don't know? So we've done all of this for nothing?"

"Hardly for nothing. Tell me what you need to do."

Christy slumped in her chair. "I don't know."

"I think you know far more than you're letting on. And if you're truly stuck, I bet you can find others willing to lend you a hand."

Turning to the class, he said, "Raise your hand if you're willing to help Christy find the answers she needs."

All of us raised our hands.

Turning back to Christy, he said, "I'll help too. Just don't expect others to have the answers for you. You'll get plenty of suggestions, probably more than you can handle, but the ultimate decision has to rest with you. Understand?"

Christy nodded.

"Now, tell me one thing you need to do to captain your team to the Championship."

Christy bit the end of her pen. "Get a decent coach I guess."

"I'm not sure a decent coach will cut it at this point, are you?"

Christy sat straighter. "No. To save us, we need an amazing coach."

"Excellent, so now add to your card:

1. Find an amazing coach

Christy wrote it down. "But how do I do that? We don't even have the budget to hire one."

"True. Since this is such an important step, and since it will have a distinct timeline and its own collection of steps, I think it merits a notecard of its own." Mr. Griffin handed her another card. "This time, write at the top:

I intend to find an amazing coach for the girls swim team by . . .

"When do you need the coach by?" Mr. Griffin asked.

"We need her already."

"How long can you give it?"

Christy thought for a moment. "I'd say no more than two weeks."

"Then write:

> I intend to find an amazing coach for the girls' swim team by November 24. To accomplish this, I will do the following steps.

"Now we're back where we started," Christy said. "I don't know what to put down."

"As you were brave enough to go first, I'm going to help you with this card. You yourself said that a good coach just won't cut it. You need an amazing coach. Tell me, who are the best swimming coaches in the world?"

"I don't know. I suppose the Olympics coaches. Or the coaches of the top college programs."

"Excellent. Start with them."

Christy shot up in her chair. "I can't do that!"

"Why not?"

"What do you want me to do, call the Russian Olympics coach and tell her I'm a high school student looking for a swim coach, and oh yeah, I have no budget to pay you, but would you help me out by coaching me for free?"

"I'd be inclined to start with the US Olympics coach rather than the Russian, but why not? Worst case, you'll get a no, which leaves you no worse off than you are now."

"I'm guaranteed to get a no, so why bother wasting my time?"

"Granted, if you call her up and yap like a whiny teenager, 'I'm looking for a coach who's willing to work for free,' then you'll get a no."

"So what do I say?"

"Don't tell her what you want her to do, tell her *why* you want her to do it."

Christy brow pinched. "I want her to do it because we need a coach."

"No, that's still what you *want her to do*." Mr. Griffin groaned. "You need to sell her on your vision."

Christy tilted her head. "How do I do that?"

"Tell me, why do you need a coach?" Mr. Griffin tapped his pen against his palm.

"So we can win."

"And what will you do if you win?"

"Dedicate the victory to Coach Silver's memory."

"Why?"

"She was an amazing coach and got killed by a drunk driver." Christy pursed her lips. "We miss her."

"That" Mr. Griffin pointed his pen at her, "is a lot more compelling than 'we want a coach for free.'"

"Yeah," Jarod said, "when you first said you wanted a new coach, I didn't care all that much. But when you stood in front of the class and dreamed up your win at State's, I got all excited for you."

Christy turned to face him. "Really?"

"For sure."

"So," Mr. Griffin said, "now can you think of what you could say to a top coach?"

"I guess I could tell her about Coach Silver and how she was killed and how we want to win State's and dedicate the win in her memory."

Jarod added, "Even I'd coach your team if you talked to me like that."

Christy smacked him on the side of the head. "You can barely even float."

"You have a powerful vision, Christy," Mr. Griffin said. "It's my experience that the best coaches love their sport and love helping others improve. Throw in a good cause, and I think you'll be surprised at how willing they'll be to help."

"That doesn't mean she'd move here from Russia to coach us," Christy said.

"Still on the Russian Olympics coach?" Mr. Griffin asked. "No, she won't move here to work with you. But you've defined success too narrowly. If you're looking for one of these coaches to quit their job and coach you instead, you're dreaming."

"But I need a coach." Christy turned her hands up. "How else could I define success?"

"Class, any of you have any thoughts?"

"I think," Darnell said, "that you could ask them if there's any help they'd be willing to give, even if it's not actually coaching you. Maybe they could give you tips or something."

"We need more than just advice at this point."

"Of course you do," Mr. Griffin said, "but Darnell's right. You don't need to get everything on the first call. The Russian Olympics coach is connected to top coaches all over the world, including some who live several thousand miles closer. She might be willing to make an introduction or even look at a video of one of your practices and give you feedback over video conference."

"You really think she'd say yes?"

"Absolutely," Mr. Griffin said. "I think there's at least a 10% chance."

Whatever light had built up in Christy's eyes went out. "Only 10%? So now we're back to nowhere."

"Not even close. Tell me, what separates great salespeople from ordinary ones?"

Christy shrugged. "I suppose it's the ability to get people to say yes."

"That's the second greatest distinction. More important is the ability to hear the word no."

"How does that help?" Jarod asked.

"Ordinary salespeople go out on a sales call, and if they get a no, they get discouraged. The great ones hear no after no and keep going. Some even tell themselves that they need to hear no ten times to get one yes. Getting a no actually excites them, as they tell themselves that it brings them closer and closer to getting a yes."

"What are you saying?" Christy asked.

"Like I told you before, each time you reach a world class coach and tell her your story, you might have a 10% chance of getting her to help you out. So if you're only willing to call one or two coaches, the odds are that you'll fail. But remember, this is a math class. What would happen to your odds if you called 20?"

"Now you want me to call 20 of the best coaches in the world?"

"A few minutes ago, when I asked you what you'd be willing to do to reach your goal, you said *anything*. Now you're telling me that making 20 phone calls is beyond you?"

"I guess not."

"Good. So on your second notecard, write down the following steps:

1. Research the top swimming coaches in the world
2. Make a list of 20 World Class Coaches to reach out to

"But here's the thing, if you call with the expectation of getting a no, they'll detect that in your voice. Before each call, you must reconnect with your vision and fully believe that you'll get a yes."

"That makes sense to me," Christy said. "Coach Silver always told us that no matter how strong our competition, we could never go into a race thinking we were going to lose."

"Excellent, then add to your card:

3. Before each call, I will reconnect with my vision and get myself into a peak state

"Peak state?"

"Yes, in an excited, high energy, positive state of being. When you're in a peak state, it's contagious. Let's add one more:

> 4. Call each coach, and be open to whatever help they offer to give

"Are you willing to do all of that?"

"Yes, Mr. Griffin."

"If you do all of that, I expect that before your two-week deadline you'll have the coaching you need. Remember to read your cards every morning and night and check off the app each time. Your 30-day commitment starts now."

The bell rang.

"Remember, all of you committed to help Christy. Homework for tonight, I want everyone researching the world's top swimming coaches. Names are good, but let's not settle for good. Go the extra mile and get Christy phone numbers as well."

* * *

The rest of the day, I couldn't get that class out of my mind. At first, Mr. Griffin had seemed like an insensitive jerk. Rather than sympathizing with Christy's situation, he attacked her. I'd done that plenty of times myself, yelling at people when I thought they were doing the wrong thing, and it only resulted in a blowup. I learned that if I wanted people to respond to me, I was better off being sympathetic. Yet, despite his attacks, Christy had shifted, and even I believed that she might be able to find herself a coach now. How had he done that?

As soon as I got home, I created a new Google Sheet entitled *The World's Top Swimming Coaches*. I immediately invited Christy, Jarod, and Darnell and gave them editorial access to the spreadsheet. Then, after a moment, I added Mr. Griffin as well. Why not? He said he'd help.

Getting a list of the top college coaches would be easy. I could download the college rankings from the past few years and look into their programs. Perhaps I'd do that if I had time. For now, I wanted to set my sights a bit higher.

After an hour and a half of work, and plenty of help from Google Translate, I managed to find not only my target's mobile phone number but her home number and email as well. I sat back and admired my work, picturing the expression on Christy's face when she saw the contact information for the Russian Olympics coach.

Get a copy of
The Size of Your Dreams

TheSizeofYourDreams.com